THE PRIME OF MS. AMERICA

THE AMERICAN WOMAN AT FORTY

by the same author

CRISIS IN CORRECTIONS
A SINGLE STANDARD
STUDENTS IN REVOLT
BLACK PRIDE
THE LONG FREEDOM ROAD

THE PRIME
OF MS. AMERICA

THE AMERICAN WOMAN AT FORTY

by *Janet Harris*

G. P. PUTNAM'S SONS
NEW YORK

FOR JOAN AND MORT
WITH LOVE

Acknowledgments

I should like to thank the many friends who helped me with this book: Mildred Irwin, who first suggested its theme; Russell Hoffman, whose knowledge and insight into behavior have been invaluable to me; Helen Stephens, for her capable assistance with the preparation of the manuscript; Ruth Brenowitz, for her generosity and patience in aiding with the research; the eighty-odd women who kindly agreed to be interviewed and to answer questionnaires. I should also like to acknowledge, with affection and gratitude, my debt to my sisters in consciousness raising—Helen, Freda, Maria, Gwen, Mildred, Reba, Mathilde, and Eileen—for sharing their feelings and experiences with me during the past two years. Thanks also to Random House for kind permission to use passages from *Portnoy's Complaint* and to Little, Brown & Co., for permission to quote from *Human Sexual Response* and *Human Sexual Inadequacy* by William H. Masters and Virginia E. Johnson.

Contents

Chapter 1

A ROLE WITHOUT A SCRIPT

Thus woman entering her sixth age of life, 40-65, stands at the border of the longest phase of all—and yet the least definable, the most poorly structured of all. During this entire time . . . she will be reasonably vigorous, healthful and even attractive, rather than prematurely withered by diseases and worn by excessive childbearing. She will be financially comfortable, and increasingly free to use her money for experiences she previously had no time for. This need not, therefore, be the anti-climax of life. In these years, many men are in their prime. . . . Perhaps it would be so with women, too, but since the problem is a new one in history, no one has thought about it much, or yet done any intelligent planning toward that end.

—MORTON HUNT, *Her Infinite Variety*

Forty. Fifty. Sixty.

Who am I?

The role comes upon each of us suddenly, unexpectedly. We have lived at least four decades—structured lives, for the most part, in which we knew what we wanted and what was expected of us. And now, suddenly, with the beginnings of the middle years, we face an identity crisis for which nothing in our past has prepared us and for which nothing in our society can provide guidelines. For the next twenty years we will find ourselves without a metaphysic, filling a role without a script, facing a future in which we have no models. And we will have a haunting fear that our society in transition—engulfed by sweeping economic, technological, demographic, political, social, and moral changes—not only does not yet know what to do with us, but has not yet acknowledged our existence.

Who am I? How did I get here?

Daughters of the middle class or the upwardly striving working classes, we were born into a secure place in the American scheme. We were to be virginal as girls, radiant as brides, fulfilled as wives and mothers. And if there were any questions, we found the answers in the media—in magazines, in books, and most pervasively in the movies.

With the road before us so clearly marked we made the journey through childhood, our teens. We dated. We washed our silky hair; we experimented with makeup. We studied the face in the cold cream ad: "She's beautiful! She's engaged! She uses Pond's." We bought the ten-cent jar and waited for the miracle.

We wore white at our weddings. We wrote thank-you notes, furnished apartments, worried about "working out a satisfactory sex adjustment." In due time we became pregnant. We shopped for layettes. We considered spinal block and natural childbirth. We had babies, postpartum blues, sleepless nights, problems with formulas. We bought houses in the suburbs, the better to rear our children.

Our children grew up; our husbands, bolstered by our encouragement, sympathy, understanding, and good cooking advanced up the ladder of success. We bought second cars, chauffeured our daughters to dancing lessons, our sons to the Cub Scouts. We worked, according to Department of Labor statistics, nearly eighty hours a week. We were busy, needed, desired, and even somewhat appreciated.

Each period in our lives had its disciplines, but one played the game according to the rules. If school was tedious, confining, the reward was a diploma, a good job. Midnight feeding and colic—the price of young motherhood was exhaustion, anxiety, boredom, but the prize made it worthwhile. We spoke of *"building* a marriage," not living it or experiencing it. We were brought up with the value that as we sow, so shall we reap. We discarded the idea that anything we did was its own reward. Existentialism was a chic word game played by Sartre and De Beauvoir in outdoor cafés in Paris; we needed to make no existential choices for ourselves.

But in spite of our unquestioning acquiescence to the values of our society—and now, in retrospect, perhaps also our lack of imagination and independence—we were not entirely fools. In our twenties and increasingly in our thirties, we knew that we were living in our halcyon years. Brought up in the puritan work ethic, we defined ourselves according to our usefulness to society as workers, breeders, guardians of the home and its morals; to our husbands as companions, homemakers, sex partners, hostesses; and to our children—whom we nurtured, educated, and prepared to replace us in the grand design. Reared as we were in a youth and beauty-oriented society, we measured ourselves by our ornamental value: Doors were opened for us; taxis ground their brakes to stop for us; truck drivers pulled off the road to change our flat tires. We had the power of our confidence in our ability to attract men and to reassure them of their potency.

Knowing that our lives were in the main good, fulfilling, rewarding, we sometimes worried about the future. "Middle age is the way you would feel about summer if you knew there would never be another spring," wrote Clare Boothe Luce in her play *The Women*. The loss of youth, strength—age etching its

marks on our faces and bodies; dread about menopause; death of parents; loss through death and
separation of friends and family; dissatisfactions in
our marriages; the "forty-year syndrome" in our
husbands; our children growing up, preparing to
leave. And then the empty nest, the empty hours.

But even sensing the specters of the future, how
could one prepare for middle age? Suddenly the
guidebook is filled with blank pages, for as each of the
complex parts we filled in the past ends, a vacuum
appears. Our expertise, our capabilities and graces in a
score of major and minor roles have equipped us for no
new place. The years in which we were essential—
when we found the "I" in "We"—are ended; our
worth is no longer to others. At forty, forty-five, fifty
we witness the crumbling of all the defenses that
society has provided for us—we hurtle off into
nothingness.

For me, the sudden shock of middle age came when
I was forty, coinciding with the breakup of my
marriage. For a time I hid from the insistent questions
that I knew had to be answered if I were to remake my
shattered life: Who am I? How did I get here? Where
do I go now? Instead, I found myself looking around
me—at women who were my friends, acquaintances,
professional associates. In this strange new place, I
felt the sharp need for communion with my sisters, to
learn from them what paths I could take to restore the
sense of purpose, the contentment that I had so
suddenly lost.

But speaking to other women, I began to perceive in
them the same groping for certainties, the sense of
being cast adrift that I thought was my unique inner

climate. Gradually I began to perceive that I had been hurtled into a territory with unmarked borders. The questions I asked echoed back to me from a sharp-witted, sophisticated editor, whose life in a fashionable New York brownstone had always seemed to me a satisfying blend of professional success, carefree travel, parties with well-known and interesting people, exciting love affairs. I heard them in the suburbs, from the wives of business executives, lawyers and doctors, from a distinguished professor of Romance languages; from a California mother of four who had recently returned to college for her long-postponed degree; from women whose sleek good looks were a tribute to the skills of their hairdressers and dressmakers; from women whose lives were devoted to community service and humanitarian causes.

The women expressed the problem in different ways. Sometimes it was almost a renunciation of the lives they had led until this point. "I never realized how little my husband and I had in common," one woman complained, "until the kids went off to college. We don't seem to have anything to talk about. Maybe we grew apart—or maybe I just never noticed that we never were really together." There was some subtle sense of having been deceived, cheated. "What's the use of sacrificing yourself for your family? They all go off and leave, and where are you? My husband has his life outside, but I have only the empty house."

Sometimes I heard regrets about marriage—after twenty-five years or so of seemingly compatible unions. Some of the women questioned their original choices: "I think I would have been happier with a different man." Several women told me they envied the independence of this new generation: "If I were twenty today, I wouldn't marry at all." The word "compromise" came up a number of times: "At this age you learn to make the best of what you have. I look around, and every marriage seems to be missing something . So I just go along, and at least I'm glad that I'm not alone."

Much of what I observed seemed to be a running from loneliness and alienation. The divorced and widowed women were on a merry-go-round of mate searching. Sometimes the feeling of being cast adrift was disguised as illness—a general malaise, a feeling of being "dragged out." Or in preoccupation with sleep patterns: "I have more and more trouble getting up every day." Or the opposite: "I wake up after about four hours, and I can't go back to sleep." Some of the women expressed their dissatisfaction with "the rut I'm in," and in the autumn of the year I was divorced, I remember hearing a half dozen brave plans from women for the revision of their lives. One woman vowed to make losing twenty-five pounds her "project." There was a sudden rash of calls to interior decorators, the collection of paint and fabric samples, as though in the remodeling of their homes or the remaking of their bodies the women could somehow find the place and the person they were seeking.

Even among the women I knew who seemed to be making the best "adjustment" to middle age, there was still the leitmotif of unfamiliarity with the new self, uncertainty about the outcome of the mode of survival they had chosen. On all fronts, danger seemed to surround them. The marriages that had seemed so secure only a few years ago were in jeopardy; my presence as a recent divorcée in the "old crowd" was a hazard—a reminder of how fragile a seemingly sound marriage might really be.

Putting together the bits and pieces of what I had heard, listening to women speak of their problems, of their floundering for solutions, I began to sense that what had happened to us was more than a transition to a new phase of life, for indeed, the nature of women's life in our society is a constant adjustment to one unrelated role after another. It was not a loss of husband or child, of even beauty and health; it was a loss of *all* the selves that each of us had been. One of my friends expressed it most poignantly: "I'm the ultimate in the throwaway society, the disposable woman."

Listening to women expressing their doubts and confusion about their own images of self, I began to wonder what the public image was. Scanning magazine ads, watching television commercials and situation comedies, checking out movies, I found out how middle age is portrayed by the media.

In the popular magazines, there is no shortage of positive images of the middle years—for *men.* The models are generally in their forties, sometimes even their fifties and sixties. Tanned, virile, they preside with dignity in walnut-paneled conference rooms; at leisure, they lounge on the decks of Bimini-bound yachts with bikini-clad teen-agers. "While you're up . . . Get me a Grant's," a craggy-faced forty-year-old calls from his typewriter to a long-haired twentyish blonde. Whatever the realities of middle age may be for a man in our society, as he is mirrored in the media, he can be a successful tycoon or a rugged outdoorsman, he can be dignified—even distinguished—and still remain a sex symbol, whose potency and desirability are attested to by the adoring look on the face of the young woman posed with him.

In contrast, one searches the magazines in vain for women past their first youth. The middle-aged face apparently sells neither perfume nor floor wax. Half-size dresses, obviously marketed to mature women, are modeled by plump, dimpled darlings in their twenties; an ad for a face cream designed for women "over thirty" features a model one suspects is still more concerned with acne than wrinkles. In the Ivory Snow ad, there is, finally, a picture of an attractive fortyish redhead. Her hands are beautiful, it seems, not because they have planted a garden, cooked a meal, comforted a sick child, or written a poem—but because they look "as young as her daughter's." The role of the mature woman in the media is almost entirely negative. Youth has glamor, and old age dignity, but the middle-aged woman is a sad joke. She is the silly clubwoman, perennial shopper, castrating female, carping mother-in-law. "Please, Mother, I'd rather do it myself," a harried young housewife screams to her interfering, domineering parent. In another television commercial a bride presents a dish of pasta to a mother-in-law, whose skeptical face would chill a cordon bleu chef. In a third, a young man berates a middle-aged woman for scratching his car door with the handle of hers and then, discovering the culprit to be a young, beautiful girl, melts and acknowledges that "it was nothing."

In the movies, the image is even worse. In recent years the middle-aged actress has gone from harridan to horror figure. Bette Davis, in actuality an accomplished, sophisticated artist, set the new scene in *Whatever Happened to Baby Jane.*

A former child star, Baby Jane, now fifty, prances around in a smocked dress, long white stockings and blond corkscrew curls, serving dead rats to her invalided sister, Joan Crawford, who it seems also is an aging villainess. In *Hush, Hush, Sweet Charlotte,* the portrait is of a middle-aged lady as a coy ax murderess. There is no distinction even in evil; the middle-aged woman is both a fiend and a fool. In fact, the image of the figure of fun is the dominant one. Mrs. Portnoy, the castrator, has the killer instinct, but in the main, she's a silly. "I haven't gained five pounds," says the superannuated seductress, "since you were born. Feel . . ." and then, archly to her husband: "Look at him looking at his mother like she's some sixty-year-old beauty queen!"

Even in the most kindly portrayal, the woman in her middle years is a simp. One thinks of the Helen Hokinson clubwomen, whom John Mason Brown describes in the preface of the book of cartoons *The Ladies, God Bless 'Em:*

> They were quite a group, these Hokinson dowagers. Funny, they certainly were. Yet they were also human, and poignant. . . . They could not bring themselves to realize that their youth had left them . . . they were girls at heart. . . . Wherever their minds may have remained parked, those tiny feet of theirs, which terminated their plump legs, were forever carrying their bodies into book stores and museums, or leading them to lectures, matinees or concerts. That is, of course, when Miss Hokinson's well-fed, well-bred, and thoroughly minked ladies were not molesting flowers, cajoling

maids, tangling traffic . . . or attempting to become sylphs again by submitting themselves to the costly Spartanism of Elizabeth Arden. . . . Their chief problem was idleness . . . they had to seek employment to fill their empty days . . . they were incessant shoppers. They were more intrigued with what covered their heads than what filled them . . . Miss Hokinson's matrons were lonely. . . . Even Philip Wylie could not have disliked these women since they were entirely innocent of Momism. They were too busy babying themselves to mother anyone else. Foolish and self-indulgent as they were, they were never guilty of meanness. They were a friendly breed. This explains why they made so many friends.

The tragedy of the middle years can be read between the lines of John Mason Brown's critique. Everyone loves the ladies, God bless them, because they are jaunty, empty-headed, and frivolously hatted—in the face of disaster. One can't criticize them: Why should the forty-year-old woman *not* baby herself, spend her days in useless activity, be a lovable parasite? *What else is there for her to do or be?*
Who am I? Where do I go from here?

The questions that had begun for me as personal ones—my own search for an identity, for purpose, for a life-style that would provide the contentment, status, and security that I had known in the past—now seemed to me to be the central ones to women of my generation. The pursuit for answers led me from my own circle of friends to the examination of my society itself, for by now my search had become a professional assignment. Again my efforts met with frustration. I had difficulty even finding an acknowledgment of the enigma that I knew was the reality of my life and that I saw mirrored in the lives of most of my contemporaries. I found that although there was an abundance of material on the problems of adolescence and on the aging, there were relatively few studies of the middle years. Baffled, I wondered what the reason was for the conspiracy of silence.

I found the solution to this first puzzle in demographic research—in studies of population characteristics compiled by the Bureau of the Census and by other government agencies. The evidence was there, in figures that had changed drastically during the past half century in birth and death rates, in brand-new patterns of mobility and stability, in radically altered figures on education and vocational attainment, in new categories of affluence and poverty, in statistics concerning family patterns, marriage and divorce. *The woman of my generation reaching her middle years is a completely new species, and if her territory is uncharted, it is no wonder!*

I learned that today a woman of forty has exactly twice as much chance of living through the next decade as she would have had in 1920. I saw that medical advances, birth control, changes in diet and living conditions not only have changed mortality figures, but contribute to making a woman of forty or fifty—in previous generations relegated to the patient acceptance of approaching old age—strong, healthy, vigorous, attractive. Middle age was once a matter of a few years spent in declining health; today it is the longest period of a woman's life.

I discovered that changing mobility rates meant new family patterns. For example, the role of grandmother is no longer likely to be an active one, for the statistics show that women in the middle years now can expect to be separated by large distances from the next two generations of their families. I learned that there is an increasing number of women who are now or who will be shortly living alone. In 1920, for instance, a woman was in her middle fifties when her last child attained majority; today the likelihood is that she will confront the empty nest when she is just past forty. I discovered that in 1920 a woman could anticipate one year of widowhood; today, if she is married to a man of her own age, she is likely to be a widow for eight years.

Economic patterns have changed. Ours is the highest income group; we are, indeed, the "New Affluents." Vocational patterns have changed; we have established a new category in the labor force—returners—workers who have allowed a twenty-year gap to separate two halves of a career. Educational statistics have changed, as have statistics describing religious, social, moral attitudes and behavior. The sum of these mutations is a new breed of women, a vast sorority of forty- to sixty-year-olds, middle-class women, whose longevity and life-style have been created by the changes that science and technology have brought during the second half of this century. We are anonymous—graphed but not acknowledged, a shadowy presence—hinted at, but never defined.

For definitions, I went to the experts. I read studies by the authorities in each field about the condition of our mental and physical health, our vocational and marriage patterns, our educational choices, our cultural interests. I consulted psychiatrists, physicians, educators, sociologists, clergymen, vocational guidance counselors, marriage counselors. I found facts, direction, a framework for this book.

Much of what I was finding out was discouraging, led me into blind alleys. But as I accumulated facts, studied surveys, evaluated statistics, I began to suspect that perhaps I had missed the very theme of this book; I could find no testimony to settle my doubts, for it seemed that the question on my mind had not been posed before. Was it possible, I wondered, that what had at first seemed to me to be nothingness, an abyss, could be instead a golden opportunity for a new life—one with options, alternatives, freedoms never open to women of my generation at any other time in their lives and never open to any other generation of women at all? *Was it possible for a woman—in the absence, for the first time in her life of demands, values, and rewards established by others— to find herself in the scattered pieces of all the parts she had played and in effect to create herself and a life to be lived on her own terms?*

I went back to the women, not just the women I knew, but now to a sizable cross section of my generation—widows, divorcées, married women, single women—with questionnaires, with interviews that lasted sometimes for many hours. I asked them what their lives had been like in the past and what their lives were like now. I questioned them about their sex lives, I asked them how they saw themselves as *women.* I asked them about their physical health, about their emotional highs and lows. I asked them about their relationships with husbands and children, with friends and lovers. I asked them whether they worked, how they saw themselves as career women, what employment offered them. I inquired about their leisure time, what books they read, what television and movie programs they saw. I asked them about their hobbies, their intellectual interests. I queried them about their evaluation of this time in their lives: Was it a period of growth, new experience? Was it a time of consolidation of life's experience? Finally, I asked them what accomplishments and satisfactions they sought, what they hoped for and planned for in the future.

This, then, is their story.

Chapter 2

MOTHERS AND DAUGHTERS

*As I was saying of her she was getting older now and her face
and the body of her gave a wooden look to her.*

*There was nothing in her to connect her with the past, the
present or the future, there was not any history of her. There were
three daughters to her and they lived altogether. . . . The only
thing that could ever give to anyone who knew her a history of
her was as they would see it in the history of each one of the three
girls who had once been inside her . . . there was never in her
any connection inside her with a past or present or a
future . . . .*

—GERTRUDE STEIN, *The Making of Americans*

One of the ways to find the answer to the existential
question "Who am I?" is through the past, for as Erik
Erikson explains, the search for identity is predicated
on finding some meaningful resemblance between
what we see ourselves to be and what others judge and
expect us to be. These expectations are part of the
history within us—the history of our mothers and
grandmothers, of the generations of women before us
whose voices echo in our conscious and unconscious
minds, setting out for us our values, our goals, the
rights and responsibilities we may take for ourselves,
declaring, through the images of them that we
remember, our own roles in life.

For us in America the search for identity through the
past is obscured. In a future-oriented society such as
ours, people are standardized not by the social roles of
the ancestors, but through a common vision of the
future. We are motivated toward bigger achievement—

the ranch house in the suburbs, the prestigious job, college for the children—not toward the perpetuation of past tradition or even the stabilization of the present. Moreover, we live now in a period of technological, political, and social change so rapid that our lives frequently bear only fragmentary relationships to those of the women who came before us. Even biological experiences cannot be shared by the generations: Giving birth in a hospital in Westchester in 1950 was nothing at all like bringing forth a baby in a slum tenement in 1910. Each generation of American woman is immigrant in time and space; we have only tenuous ties to the worlds of the women before us.

But despite the fact that our society requires each generation to cut out an identity from new cloth, we bear upon us the imprint of our heritage. The lessons we learned at mother's knee may seem irrelevant to the present—"Times are different, now, Mother," we explain patiently, defending our permissiveness toward our children—but we still measure ourselves against them. We *wish* to divorce ourselves from the past—"I wouldn't want my life to be like my mother's" was a statement I heard over and over again in researching this book—but we cannot cut it loose. It molded us, formed us, returns to haunt us and sometimes even to expand our concepts of what *should* be—and it bears looking into.

Who were the women in our past? We come from a divergent group, we of the middle class and middle years in America. Some of our parents were immigrants, bringing to America the culture of the old country. Some of us are descended from pioneer stock, the men and women who settled a frontier and established the dominant patterns in America that prevailed in the last century. A few of us are "old stock," with our roots in Colonial America. But each of us, growing up, moved in two worlds: that of her intimate family and the greater one, the melting pot of America itself, in which the elements of other cultures blended into the prevailing mores of the era.

The likely place to begin a search for the mores and roles of the past is in literature. The economic, political, legal status of women has been accurately recorded; we know that under English common law women in America enjoyed no legal rights; that Abigail Adams, in a letter to her husband, soon-to-be-president John Adams, warned:

> In the new code of laws which I suppose it will be necessary for you to make, I desire you would remember the ladies, and be more generous and favorable to them than your ancestors. . . . If particular care and attention is not paid to the ladies, we are determined to foment a rebellion, and will not hold ourselves bound by any laws in which we have no voice or representation.

We know that the first women's rights movement, probably stemming from the work of Mary Wollstonecraft in England at the beginning of the nineteenth century, set as its goals the legal emancipation of women, their rights to equal education and work; that the suffrage movement, under the leadership of Lucy Stone and Elizabeth Cady Stanton, in the middle of the nineteenth century, called for granting to women property and civil rights and eventually the vote. We know that women in the nineteenth century were, in effect, legally chattels; that they had no rights to own property, sue or be sued in court, or even have custody of their children; that the doors of colleges and universities were closed to them; that they were, in the larger world, second-class citizens.

But history tells us little about family life; for the role of women in their everyday existence, we must look into novels, journals, diaries. From these sources a different picture emerges: American life was somewhat androgynous—that is to say, there were not significant differences in the goals, satisfactions, achievements of men and women. A scarcity of labor in a predominantly agrarian society where home crafts were the primary form of industry spawned a kind of rough equality between the sexes and the generations and made the home a self-contained unit. No member of any household was surplus. There was no need to create roles, nor did the years bring abrupt change and termination of usefulness. Adulthood came early—a child was a contributing member of the family at eight or nine, and life flowed along a steady course into middle age and eventually old age. The identity crises at each point were resolved within the framework of the knowledge of one's usefulness during all of one's life.

Retrospect lends a rosy light; as we look backward, it is easy to idealize the good old days. "The West Wasn't Won with a Registered Gun," reads the National Rifle Association's bumper sticker, instantly evoking nostalgic pictures of strong, broad-shouldered men forging a frontier in a blaze of righteous gunfire. Likewise, there is the romantic vision of the pioneer wife, her sunbonnet tied under her firm little chin, her steady gaze on the westward horizon, dauntless in the face of Indian massacres and drought, bringing comfort and domesticity to a wilderness. Sorting out the past, we see the grimmer side of the past: O.E. Rolvaag's epic *Giants in the Earth* gives us the stark reality of life on the frontier. His heroine, Beret, the wife of Per Hansa, a Norwegian immigrant who homesteaded on the Dakota prairie, was never able to find a self-identity even in a society where one's role was carefully proscribed; we see her brooding in her sod hut, afraid of the hard responsibilities, physical dangers, and loneliness of her life, escaping her own thoughts as she turns for comfort to a dark religion, and finally descending into periodic schizophrenia.

Allowing for the fact that individual capacities for happiness vary, that in each generation there are those who find life rewarding and those to whom it is a tragedy, and that looking backward always brings the temptation to succumb to idealization, there is still convincing evidence that within the framework of women's role there were at one time possibilities for creativity and fulfillment that somehow have been lost to us today. There is some clear evidence that there has been in recent times a sharp cutoff from the past, a cataclysmic change in the roles of both men and women and most specifically in the role of women past their childbearing years. It is this change that is the key to the way that we as mature women now view our lives and the way in which we fit into the general outlines of our society.

The evidence emerges with brilliant clarity in a comparison of two novels, the first, *The Rise of Silas Lapham* by William Dean Howells, a story of the rise of the capitalist class in America just after the Civil War, and the second, Sinclair Lewis's classic about the

American twenties, *Babbitt.* Here are portraits of two ladies, born a half century apart:

. . . Mrs. Lapham, while keeping a more youthful outline, showed the sharp print of the crow's foot at the corners of her motherly eyes, and certain slight creases in her wholesome cheeks. . . . Lapham was proud of his wife; she encouraged and helped him from the first, and bore her full share of the common burden. She had health, and she did not worry her life out with peevish complaints and vagaries; she had sense and principle, and in their simple lot she did what was wise and right. . . . No one gave up more than they when they gave up each other when Lapham went to the war. When he came back and began to work, her zeal and courage formed the spring of his enterprise.

Myra Babbitt—Mrs. George F. Babbitt—was definitely mature. She had creases from the corners of her mouth to the bottom of her chin, and her plump neck bagged. But the thing that marked her as having passed the line was that she no longer had reticences before her husband, and no longer worried about not having reticences. She was in a petticoat now, and corsets which bulged, and unaware of being seen in bulgy corsets. She had become so fully habituated to married life that in her full matronliness she was as sexless as an anemic nun. She was a good woman, a kind woman, a diligent woman, but no one, save perhaps Tinka, her ten-year-old, was at all interested in her or entirely aware that she was alive.

Individual differences? Yes, undoubtably. But still, from what one knows of the past, it is virtually impossible to place Myra Babbitt in any earlier period of history. Her life is one of gray anonymity, purposelessness—she is a "comparatively movable part of the furniture," who describes her daily routine as meaningless activity, "'ordering three meals a day, three hundred and sixty-five days a year,'" who wails that she ruins her eyes "'over that horrid sewing machine . . . and the laundry,'" and whose final question as she awaits surgery alone in a hospital room is: "'I was wondering if anybody really needed me, or wanted me. I was wondering what was the use of my living.'" The picture, in chilling contrast with that of Mrs. Lapham, serene in the knowledge of her own worth and her value to others, seems so curiously modern.

Who am I? How did I get here?

Let's go backward and trace our steps, this time through the media. Among my souvenirs there is a copy of the *Ladies' Home Journal*, August, 1919. The magazine is nearly the size of a tabloid newspaper. One envisions it on a wicker table on a porch furnished with cretonne-covered settees and hanging baskets of fern; the cover, in fact, announces that it is the "Summer Porch Number." Leafing through its pages, one sees clearly the woman in whose ample lap the magazine will repose:

She is a mature woman. The fashion pages' models are full-bosomed and wide-hipped. An article written by the "Plain Country Woman" finds it "absurd" to "dress up in finery" to give the illusion of youth; it "even wears on men and impresses them with fearful ennui and disillusion." A woman preserves her beauty by "going on with the business of life as it presents itself day-to-day. . . . Let us discard mere prettiness for beauty of heart and mind, which more than anything smooth the path to old age and add charm to the face from which the bloom of youth has fled." The "bloom of youth" generally gets little coverage; not only is it not worshiped, envied, or regretted in its loss, but it is a bit pitiable. The millinery page is given over to the "new moon bonnets"—a malines cap trimmed with bands of "gold lace applique," and a "fascinating cap for the evening motor ride," but the young faces that model the creations are sweetly vacuous and, for all their rosy cheeks and ruby lips, as unappealingly fragile as wax dolls.

She is the preserver of new life. There are constant reminders of the high infant mortality of the time: "In the long nights of sorrow, many a mother has said again and again, 'Was there anything that I could have done to save my baby?'" reads the copy for Nestle's Baby Food. The Colgate's Talc Powder ad reassures mother that the product has "just the right proportion of boric acid and other sanitive ingredients."

She is preserver of the continuity of life. The young mother in the Ivory Soap ad bathes her baby under the tender and watchful eye of her own mother. "A quarter-century ago grandma's mother told her how to bathe a new baby girl. . . . Today she, in turn, passes on the same instructions to that girl, now a mother, herself."

She is educator, guardian of morality, uplifter of taste. "Do not send your child to school before he is 10 years old if you can possibly teach him to read, write and cipher." The article lays out a home-teaching plan that includes directions for teaching Longfellow's "Hiawatha" to a five-year-old. Another, which shows photographs of young men and women performing calisthenics at the beach—the men in one-piece knee-length bathing suits, the young ladies in billowing bathing dresses and long black stockings—asks, "How much of this do you want your daughter to share—or even see?"

She is a self-realizer. The most illuminating story in the magazine is called "My Life with a Pat of Butter" and reflects the sixty-year struggle of the narrator to fulfill herself and carry out her responsibilities to others. She writes of her struggles to go to college, to attain the chairmanship of "a department at an Eastern College," and then, after losing her sister and brother-in-law in one of the nameless winter plagues of the time, her decision to sacrifice her career to rear their seven children. Devoting all her "brain power and energy to the scientific study of farming," she achieves financial success. Watching the children "growing to manhood and womanhood," fortified by her having "instilled in them the self-respect that independence alone engenders," she makes plans to sell the farm and retire in peace and serenity to the "high cultural atmosphere" of the college town she had abandoned.

Leafing through the pages, one sees the World War I woman in all her aspects. Duty and devotion to husband and family did not require her to forgo yearnings for adventure; there is a hair-raising account by an intrepid lady named Dora Keen on "How I Climbed a 14,000 Foot Mountain in the Dead of Winter." Courage, in fact, was a woman's estate; "The First Woman Born in the West" describes a girlhood that featured famine, "howling wolves," and Indian massacres. Additionally, she was idealistic, concerned with the welfare and improvement of humanity: Jane

Addams, the founder of the settlement movement in
America, and Ida Tarbell, the muckraking author, each
had a page in the *Journal.* She was deeply religious;
there are no fewer than three articles about religion.

Who, then, was the woman on the porch? She was
wife, mother, nurturer, passer of the torch, adventurer,
self-creator, career woman possibly, scholar, conveyer
of culture. She found her identity in a life given
purpose by its responsibilities and pleasure by its
accomplishments and achievements.

What she was not was—*disposable.*

The modern woman did not emerge gradually; she
seems to have sprung, nearly full-formed, from the
revolution in manners and morals that took place in
the decade following the First World War. A walk up
any street in America in, say, 1924, would have told
the story. The woman on the porch—the ideal of only a
decade earlier, her demeanor and dress conveying
fruitful maturity and ripened wisdom—might as well
have been swept away by a tidal wave. In her place
was a slender, leggy, short-skirted creature, with
flattened breasts, lips painted to suggest charming
petulance, eyebrows plucked to an arc of insolent
sauciness. "The women of this decade worshipped
youth," writes Frederick Lewis Allen in his history of
the twenties, *Only Yesterday.* "They wanted to be
men's casual and lighthearted companions . . . their
irresponsible playmates." The "broadhipped mother
of the race" became passé almost overnight; in her
stead was a "child-woman."

The flapper as replacement for the woman on the
porch was a symbol of the upheaval of American
values and ideals that took place during World War I.

The shock of the war, plunging the world into a worldwide barbarism unknown since the era of Attila the Hun, brought the loss of innocence to a whole society. It ended what Allen calls the "humdrum routine of American life . . . the moral dicta . . . the Pollyanna land of rosy ideals. . . . A whole generation was caught up in the eat-drink-and-be-merry-for-to-morrow-we-die spirit which accompanied the departure of the soldier to the training camps and fighting fronts."

American morality—reverence for sexual virtue, hard work, thrift, honesty, devotion to wholesome pleasures of hearth and home—withered under the stress of war emergencies. The sheltering, nurturing, nonsexual woman of the prewar period was obsolete. None of her values, it now seemed, really served to preserve stability, order, or even life itself. The new woman was a devil-may-care temptress, who understood that life was transitory, to be savored for the moment; her function was to offer respite from panic with a teasing flip of her short skirt. Brett Ashley, the heroine of Hemingway's *The Sun Also Rises*, with her cynical promiscuity, Iris March, in Michael Arlen's *A Green Hat*, whose short life was spent on the razor's edge of bootleg liquor and fast cars, were the kinds of women that men returning from the war would choose as wives and that young girls would select as role models.

The changes engendered by the war were the beginning, the first spasm in the upheaval that was to shake America. "Pollyanna land" was shortly to be swept away anyway, in the building and technological boom and the changing demography of the twenties. The process that had begun with the Industrial

Revolution was accelerated; mass production went into high speed; a new point of mechanical and managerial efficiency was reached. The industrial genius of Ford revolutionized industry; the stock market boomed; technological man was born.

The industrial man became a cog in a machine. The American translation of Renaissance man—"Jack of all trades"—became obsolete. Men were no longer craftsmen; they were no longer required to be resourceful, independent. In fact, those very qualities were handicaps in the increasingly industrial, technological, organization-oriented society, where proper functioning required the ability to be "one of the team." Men no longer had to tame the elements in any real or symbolic sense; what they had to do was conform and consume, not create or challenge. *No longer heroes, they neither needed nor wished for heroines as wives.*

While the technological revolution of the twenties brought the *modification* of men's role, in a very real sense, it *obliterated* aspects of the role of women. A major turn toward industrial expansion involved the consumer market. To spur consumerism, there was a new credit philosophy: Pay as You Go. By the early twenties, installment buying accounted for 15 percent of all sales. With the rise in product consumption, there came the expansion of services. It was no longer an American value for women to be thrifty, for the housewife to produce for her family's use. Allen reviews some of the changes:

> Women were learning how to make lighter work of the preparation of meals. Sales of canned food were growing . . . bakeries, commercial laundries, electric washing-machines and irons. . . . The

housewife was learning to telephone her shopping orders, to get her clothes ready-made . . . to buy a vacuum cleaner and emulate the lovely carefree girls in the magazine advertisements who banished dust with such delicate fingers.

The houses that the carefree girls dusted, too, were changing. Technology brought urbanization; with urbanization came smaller, compact houses and apartment living. The old homesteads with spare rooms for other generations began to disappear. The nuclear family with its proscribed complement of one mother, one father, and, say, two children became, for the first time in history, the domestic norm. Mother no longer instructed daughter on how to bathe the baby, nor for that matter, how to grow old with grace and dignity; Mother was off on her own, and so was daughter.

If the woman on the porch had already become morally passé, she was now technologically obsolete. A machine could do everything better than she. An assembly line prepared her food; a rotary motor beat her rugs. America entered the age of the specialist. Modern woman no longer healed the sick—it was the job of the doctor. She no longer educated her children—the schools provided not only instruction, but services as well: nurses, hot lunches, guidance counselors. Beyond that, she was no longer of any real use to her mate in ways that were familiar in the past; rather than a helpmeet, she was now in danger of becoming a competitor, for if he were to flounder in the baffling new society while she remained useful, the balance required in the interrelationship between men and women would be destroyed.

The pieces of the jigsaw begin to come together: the free and easy morality of the war emergency; the end to the role of men as tamers of the frontier and the substitution of mechanical man for his earlier model; the mushrooming consumer market that, in changing work habits, curtailed the utility of women as adults and partners. Add to that one more factor—what Edna Ferber called the "strange ideas of a Viennese doctor"—and we have the outlines of today's female role model.

Paralleling the cataclysmic changes in technology during the first half of the twentieth century were the inroads made into the unexplored territory of man's physical and emotional behavior. Central to this development was the work of Sigmund Freud, whose brilliant observations of human personality provided the cornerstone on which modern psychiatric and psychological theory is based. At the root of Freudian theory is his insight into the nature of sexual repression; in effect, the final result of the application of the understanding of the Oedipal conflict was the granting to both men and women rights to their own sexuality.

The problem was that the nature of female sexuality, as defined by Freud, permitted the interpretation that was to gain credence in the next decades. While Freud acknowledged that the "hysterical" women whom he analyzed were paying the price of sexual repression, he was himself a man of his times, a post-Victorian who was unable to come to grips with the schism between what his own discoveries about women told him and what the society's social and moral values imposed upon him. "What is it women really want?" he wrote in anguish, discarding the evidence that told him women wanted full adulthood. Ultimately, through his popularizers, Freud's definition of femininity came to be defined as passivity; "I do not need a comrade-at-arms," he wrote to his fiancee, Martha Bernays, instructing her to accept her role as eternal child.

The childlike image, then, was the emerging one requiring a truncated ideal. For all her life-giving virtues, the pre-World War I woman was not sexual; she was, in fact, neuter. For the American woman coming into maturity in the twenties, there was no pattern of demeanor, behavior, dress—in short, no sexual image to emulate. The closest one could come was to adopt the contours of adolescence—a time at which the biological function itself is concerned with sexual promise. Since there was no outline for fulfillment, the model had to take on the accouterments of the perpetual tease. The Woman as Adolescent emerged.

Scott Fitzgerald's heroines played at life and particularly at sex. The Jazz Age Baby sneaked snorts from a hip flask, like a willful child with a hand in the cookie jar. She rolled her stockings, left off her underwear, refused to buckle her galoshes. She lived for the moment, made no promises she intended to keep—least of all, promises toward her own future, for there was none.

Like Peter Pan, the woman of the twenties was never to grow old. In fact, she was never even to mature. Like Peter's, her world was magic. She was a sprite, living in clouds of illusion, which the media—books, magazines, and the new molder of public opinion, the cinema—was to play upon. Reality was gone; make-believe was all. The 1919 Listerine advertising campaign told women: "The prompt application of Listerine may prevent a minor accident from becoming a major infection." In 1929 it captioned a pastel of a lovelorn twenty-year-old with the words "Spring! for everyone but her . . ."

The end to illusion came with the stock-market crash in 1929. Suddenly the magic-child creature was a frivolous luxury; there was a need once again for women to be resourceful, to function as full adults. Fashions changed; the flapper look was replaced with the modest mid-calf skirt of the thirties; the boyish bosom gave way to contours that were downright matronly, but still, the child-woman of the twenties never really vanished. The past had been obliterated, and there were no real clues for a course of behavior for women.

The confused priorities of the time come into view in retrospect through motion pictures. The heroines of the thirties were the movie queens, whose lives provided an outlet for escape into vicarious glamor. After a day on her feet as a salesclerk, in a job taken to compensate for her husband's diminished paycheck, a woman was likely to spend the evening at the movies (choosing Bank Night or Free Dinnerware Night) laughing at Jean Arthur as the poor little rich girl, charmingly coping with the exigencies of a servantless twenty-room Park Avenue apartment.

American women went into the job market in increasing numbers during the Depression; they educated their daughters, when they could, with a view toward practical adulthood, but the images remained confused. In the depths of the Depression the controversy remained: Should women work? Was not every man's ideal the little woman he could "take care of"? The screen's heroes manfully asserted that *they* wore the pants; Daddy's little girl—remember *It Happened One Night*—was still expected to be adorably flutter-brained. Reviewing the literature of the day, two women stand out as womanly in the older sense—the heroine of Pearl Buck's *The Good Earth* and Ma Joad, in *The Grapes of Wrath*—but neither was a middle-class American woman.

In the midst of the general confusion about woman's role during the thirties, there was one singularly clear model for the mature woman: Eleanor Roosevelt. While her role was in one sense the traditional woman's one, "mothering" in the larger sense—the underprivileged minorities, the poor, children—it also required the energy, aggression, and strong ego that are not part of the maternal cast. The child-woman was entirely missing from Eleanor Roosevelt's image; it is virtually impossible to visualize her as having displayed any interest in vanity. Her areas of self-improvement were centered on overcoming physical and psychological handicaps—shyness and a poor speaking voice—in order to carry out her public responsibilities. Inherent in her character were the hard-core American values of courage, individuality, concern for others. Even the business in which she invested her own money—a cooperative that manufactured furniture—was so close to the pioneer style that she reiterated and translated into a modern idiom the values of the past. She was a link between the old days and the future; with one world dead and the new one not yet born, Eleanor Roosevelt provided some view of the way in which women could transcend the stunted role in which they had been placed.

The First Lady's durability as a role model was the

result of the social and political realities of the time. As we hurtled from the Depression into the Second World War, the demands for adulthood in women increased. If the Depression woman was required to take her place as a contributor, or at least a partner in adversity, the woman who came to maturity during the Second World War was even more neccessary to domestic well-being. With 16,000,000 men (out of a total population of less than 150,000,000) in military service, not only the maintenance of the home but production in industry became women's responsibilities. Before 1940 fewer than 1 in 4 women worked—a figure that had not noticeably increased since 1900 when it was 20.8 percent of the total work force. With the beginning of the war the percentage of women in industry took a swift upward turn. But more than that, the woman coming of age during the Second World War was expected to be concerned with the greater world, rather than one within the confines of home and family, an example certainly clearly set by Eleanor Roosevelt.

Looking at the woman in the first half of the 1940's, we see first the changing position she now had in her own domain. Myra Babbitt, for example, would have found her world far wider than the shopping excursions to the neighborhood Piggly Wiggly (she did not drive a car), the bridge club, and her supervision of the cleaning woman. Her preoccupation would have been with her teen-age son, rapidly approaching draft age—a reality problem that would have dwarfed the minor frustrations of life. It is possible that she might have actually been head of the household—a reserve officer was subject to Army service even past age forty. Mrs. Babbitt might have heeded her government's plea to return to industry, for war production demanded every available hand, or at the very least, she would have been engaged in volunteer work. The cleaning woman herself might leave for a job in a "defense industry"; the problems of coping with food shortages and ration books alone would have altered the household arrangements.

But beyond that, the "toy" woman of earlier years was out of style. Even the movie heroines changed; we went from Mary Pickford, she of the little-girl golden ringlets and dimpled knees, through Clara Bow, the teasing "It Girl" ("It" meant "sex" to that self-conscious generation), to the smart, sophisticated image ideals of the forties: Katharine Hepburn, Rosalind Russell, Joan Crawford—career women mainly, independent, worldly-wise, successful, capable of functioning on their own without men. The sex symbol in general was outmoded; except for the famous pinup of Betty Grable, her perfect behind turned toward the camera, peering coyly over her shoulder at the thousands of GI's who wistfully hung her picture on their barracks walls, we are hard put to remember one during the war years. With men in service, women turned their concerns to matters beyond manhunting and trapping. Rosie the Riveter was the breadwinner; women managed the financial as well as the domestic needs in the home. In industry, they were entrusted not only with men's work, but as producers of war matériel—munitions, planes, tanks—with the responsibility for men's lives as well. For the four years of the war, America was a woman's country, and the woman was a grown-up.

It is a truism in the women's movement that values, goals, life-styles for women in American society change just often enough to prevent each new generation of women from identifying with any previous ones. The independent, self-reliant woman of the forties, created by the exigencies of the time, was again about to be replaced. Betty Friedan, in her cogent analysis of the period, outlines the zeitgeist:

> There was, just before the feminine mystique took hold in America, a war, which followed a depression and ended with the explosion of an atom bomb. After the loneliness of war and the unspeakableness of the bomb, against the frightening uncertainty, the cold immensity of the changing world, women as well as men sought the comforting reality of home and children. . . . We were all vulnerable, home-sick, lonely, frightened. A pent-up hunger for marriage, home and children was felt simultaneously by several different generations; a hunger, which, in the prosperity of postwar America, everyone could suddenly satisfy.

How we, the women whose lives are the subject of this book—the youngest of whom came into the estate of womanhood during the late 1940's—equipped as we were with only the fragmented lessons of the past, denied a consistent vision of womanhood, alienated by changing culture from the generations who had spawned us, accommodated ourselves to the demands of the time and delineated our own roles as women constitutes the next lap in the journey toward the place in which we now find ourselves.

Chapter 3

ONE OF THE GIRLS

I discovered a strange thing, interviewing women of my own generation over the past ten years. When we were growing up, many of us could not see ourselves beyond the age of twenty-one. We had no image of our own future, of ourselves as women.

—BETTY FRIEDAN, *The Feminine Mystique*

Like Portnoy's, my first memories are of the time when I was new and full of wonder at my mother's magic potency, at her power even to defy the natural laws that I had just begun to observe. My first recollection: I, a four-year-old, am walking with her up a steep hill, helping her push the baby carriage that holds my brother. The cold wind has me bent nearly double. I complain to her. "Throw your shoulders back and take a deep breath," she instructs. I do, and marvelously, I stop shivering, the air loses its knife sharpness. Under her direction, I have warmed the March wind.

The fact is, like other women of her background, she *was* powerful. She defied her immigrant family by going to high school—working nights in a biscuit factory to help support her younger brother and sisters—and then to college and finally to law school. The man she married, my father, returned from the Argonne with a Purple Heart, took a law degree, established a successful Manhattan practice. Between them they achieved the American dream: two children, a house in the suburbs, a car, vacation trips to

California. For my brother and me there was or-
thodontia, summer camp, brother 'n' sister navy blue
reefers, music lessons. My mother's values, passed on
to us, included community service, civic responsibility, charitable endeavors; she was PTA president,
air-raid warden; she served on committees and
organized war relief.

My mother had worked until I was born, returned
again part time to my father's office during the
Depression, and most likely would have gone back full
time after her children were grown had she survived
the cancer that killed her at forty-four. For all her
acquisition of the accouterments of the comfortable
suburban life, she was no devotee of home and hearth.
She had marched in suffrage parades in her teens; she
worked actively in liberal political causes, set high
educational and vocational goals for her children,
particularly her daughter, whom she recognized as
ambitious. I was encouraged to enter my "composi-
tions" in writing contests, perform in school plays,
stand at the head of my class. She bought me
notebooks in which I was to write my poems,
faithfully took me on excursions to museums and
galleries, discussed the merits of local and out-of-town
colleges. If there were to be a husband and children in
my future, it was understood that would not be my first
purpose; I responded, like Jean Stafford, by dreaming
of the day when I would ride in an open car while
crowds threw roses at me. Achievement, success, fame,
a life of my own were ahead; the last occupation I ever
had in mind was housewife.

But the outside world—that of my friends ("peer
group" hadn't come into style then), the movies, the
schools—modified the values I had learned at home,

socialized me to a different reality. Success in school was not, as my mother had taught me, predicated on being smart or even studying hard. It was a precarious adjustment to mindless institution behavior. The important things were even margins and a neat handwriting. It was terribly important to remember to take one's blue-bloomered gym suit home periodically, at least once or twice a semester, and bring it back, neatly washed and ironed, in a brown paper bag. There were absence excuses, late excuses, notes excusing one from gym when one had "the curse." There were midterms and finals, and in time I understood that hardly anything I ever learned in school would be of the slightest use to me once I was graduated—an assumption borne out by the fact that although I "took" geometry steadily from my sophomore through my senior year, never to this day have I found use for one of those painfully memorized theorems.

More important were the social accommodations. There was, of course, a faceless escort, a magic Prince Charming in my daydreams, on whose arm I would attend opening nights. But in the meantime, if one was to go to parties, football rallies, proms, and the movies on Saturday nights, one had to get along with the fuzzy-faced boys who tried to "snap" one's bra in the school halls. It seemed they didn't like girls who "competed"; I learned to lose at games, to "draw them out" while they talked endlessly and boringly about football and themselves, to pretend that good grades, or any achievement for that matter, was luck, not ability. It was necessary to be very, very popular, and a 94 in chemistry certainly wasn't the answer.

Boys liked girls who were "well groomed," according to the magazines. I worried about BO, gargled with Listerine, bought little tins of Mum with my allowance money. I shaved my legs secretly with my father's Remington. I wrote to Max Factor of Hollywood for a makeup kit containing a tiny packet of powder and a minute lipstick "coordinated" to my "individual coloring." (One of the women I interviewed for this book told me she even sent away for a sample of Absorbine Jr., in case it was athlete's foot that was keeping her from being prom queen. "I would have drunk it," she told me.)

All this leads, of course, to sex. As the daughter of a "modern" college-educated woman, I had fared better than most of my friends in regard to early sex education. In answer to my questions about how babies got here, posed steadily from the age of five, my mother gave me appropriate and reasonably honest answers; by the time I was nine I pretty much had the whole picture, which I promptly shared with the rest of the neighborhood. The moral lesson I learned at home went something like this: Sex between a husband and wife was "beautiful," but only "tramps" let boys "get fresh" before they were married. It was a sort of status thing. Comparing my standards with those of my friends, I found that some of them had religious reasons for virginity—sex was "sinful"—but most of us leaned more toward the opinion that sex was "dirty" or "disgusting" in those early puberty days. At any rate, it all seemed to end the same way; by the time we were fourteen or so we all knew that boys were only out "for one thing," and a girl's job was to play it as close to the line as possible.

The game was marked off into squares: There was "necking" (acceptable), "soul kissing" (exciting, dangerous), and petting, which was subdivided, "above the waist" and "below the waist." The last two were beyond the pale; at hen parties one could confess that a boy "tried," but never that he succeeded. The losers in the game were those poor things who got "bad reputations," or conversely, the ones whom we labeled "prude," who rarely got to school dances, the "teases" who were somewhat admired by the girls, but in mortal danger of being "slapped around" by the righteous boys to whom they gave "stomach cramps" or, more forthrightly, "blue balls." The trick, of course, was to stay very, very popular without "going all the way."

Like most girls of my generation, I managed to graduate from high school with my virginity intact. I did not have to struggle against my own sexual urges—are girls nonsexual for biological reasons or do society's prohibitions hold them back? I still do not know. I do know that I felt only the faintest stirrings of desire with the boys with whom I experimented in the back seats of cars and theater balconies. Their sloppy "soul kisses," delivered while I worried about whether the Listerine really worked, bore little resemblance to my wildly erotic fantasies. The actuality of sex—or rather "sex play"—was disappointing; I knew that lust had inspired Petrarch to sonnets, had lost Troy, and had delivered England over to Luther, but I couldn't really see why. I was seventeen and finished with my freshman year at college before, lying with my own true love in the weeds, I felt my own heat rise, and I was astounded.

But sex *was* worth something; it was sheer power. Cabs screeched to a halt for me; men carried my suitcase through Penn Station's waiting room; shoe clerks found extra ration tickets for me. Like Scarlett O'Hara, I knew I had only to flutter my eyelashes and the world was mine.

The power was held in abeyance, somewhat; I was a college freshman in 1945, and the men were at war. I actually became interested in my studies, enough to go beyond the manipulative skill of knowing what a teacher wanted regurgitated on a test. I perceived that even at the land-grant Midwestern college I attended, I was among a community of scholars, and I saw what it was that my mother had found valuable in education. Scholarship, for the first time, was its own reward.

The conflicts reemerged when the war ended, and the campus again began to swarm with young men. I had taken a semester off to work as a copy girl for a New York newspaper; I returned to find the college— and for that matter the country—in the throes of postwar changes.

My recollection of the mood that had suddenly swept over all of us was the feeling of having to make up for lost years. The boys returning to college were in their twenties; those going back to jobs were ostensibly to start at the place in which they left off. There was among everyone I knew a frenzied need to push ahead.

At the university I attended, like others all over the country, the GI Bill opened the possibility of education to the masses. The young men returning from the wars were children of the Depression. Having grown up in hard times, many of them from working-class families or even homes that had been on public assistance, they viewed a diploma as the key to financial success. Off the campus business was booming; there were jobs for the asking. We were witnessing the beginning of what Clark Kerr of the University of California was to describe as the "new role of the university." "The industrial, democratic and scientific revolutions have gradually moved in on the universities and changed them almost beyond recognition. . . . The university is called upon to educate previously unimagined numbers of students; to respond to the expanding claims of national service; to merge its activities with industry as never before."

The purpose of education was to teach one to make a living. On our campus, liberal arts were out; business economics were in. Philosophy was a "bullshit" course. Accounting was not. Scouts from General Motors and Proctor and Gamble descended on the campus every spring, taking "suites" in the turn-of-the-century hotel that accommodated traveling salesmen and visiting parents, to recruit the cleanest-cut male seniors. Every graduate had his eye on the gold ring: "junior executive" with a blue-chip firm.

What place were women to take in this brave new world? Our positions were as clearly defined as the men's. Betty Friedan explains it in *The Feminine Mystique*:

> The young G.I., made older than his years by the war, could meet his lonely need for love and mother by re-creating his childhood home. Instead of dating many girls until college and profession were achieved, he could marry on the G.I. Bill. . . . Then there were the slightly older men; men of twenty-five whose marriages had been postponed by the war and who now felt they must make up for lost time; men in their thirties, kept first by depression and then by war from marrying, or if married, from enjoying the comforts of home.

For the girls, these lonely years added an extra urgency to their search for love. Those who married in the thirties saw their husbands off to war; those who grew up in the forties, were afraid, with reason, that they might never have the love, the homes and children which few women would willingly miss. When the men came back, there was a headlong rush into marriage. The lonely years when husbands or husbands-to-be were away at war—or could be sent away at a bomb's fall—made women particularly vulnerable to the feminine mystique. They were told that the cold dimension of loneliness which the war had added to their lives was the necessary price they had to pay for a career, for any interest outside the home. The mystique spelled out a choice—love, home, children or other goals and purposes in life. Given such a choice, was it any wonder that so many American women chose love as their whole purpose?

The statistics tell the story. For the first time in American history, more girls married between the ages of fifteen and seventeen than at any other age. The number of American women with three or more children doubled in twenty years; the number of children born to teen-agers rose 165 percent between 1940 and 1957. The annual rate of population increase in America outstripped India's.

In fleshing out the outlines sketched by statistics, I find the memories come rushing back. There were the surface props of collegiate life: the football games, homecoming proms. There were sorority and fraternity rushing, the Thank-God-It's-Friday party at Opal's, where we drank 3.2 beer and played the jukebox. But a deadly seriousness underlay the frivolity. There was no stag line at the dances; the returning vets claimed those long-haired girls in the sloppy joes, "pinned" them, or gave them tiny chip diamonds. Everyone was afraid to lose out in the rush.

If girls during the Depression had braved competition for jobs, mapped out careers for themselves, looked ahead to getting as firm a footing as possible on the unsteady terrain of the time, the postwar mood changed all that. The degree to be obtained, we joked, was M.R.S., soon to be supplanted by P.H.T.—"putting husband through." Co-eds returned after summer vacation with the wide gold wedding bands that had not been in fashion since the turn of the century (what stability, what seriousness of purpose those rings spelled out!) to hastily built "apartments" in Quonset huts shared with GI husbands. The campus bloomed with baby carriages; supermarkets replaced sorority houses as community gathering places. By the time I was graduated—married, of course, and making jokes about hanging my diploma over my kitchen sink— there were nine men to every girl matriculating at my college, and it was understood that a woman's place was established firmly in the home.

My diploma was obtained—and temporarily put into retirement—in 1950; a year later I was a young Westchester matron, involved full time in "creative homemaking." At the time, in making what Betty Friedan has called "the mistaken choice"—trading individuality and independence for security—it seemed that I was doing the right and natural thing. Certainly I was no maverick; all around me I saw other young women devoting themselves to domesticity, fecundity. In retrospect, the wonder grows; what was it in our backgrounds, in those "formative years" that made us *all* so susceptible to the seduction of the feminine mystique?

Interviewing women for this book, I asked for clues to check out my own experiences and memories. My questionnaire asks my interviewees information about their aspirations, about how they viewed the role of womanhood as girls. I asked them to tell me about their mothers, as they remembered them in their childhood: "Did she seem to you to be happy?" .I asked. "How did she speak about being a woman? What were your impressions of *her* life, at the time *you* were in your teens, early twenties? Did you want to emulate it?" I asked women to tell me about themselves as they were between the ages of fourteen and twenty-two. About their plans for a career, for marriage, for family. I asked them how they visualized themselves then at thirty, at forty—how they saw themselves in the future.

The answers, not surprisingly, show a wide diversity. My friends and I were the daughters of the "emancipated" post-World War I woman; some of the women I interviewed, who were ten or so years older than I, were born to women who instilled in them the "old-style" values. "My mother told me to find a good man—and take care of him," one woman wrote succinctly. "In our family it was understood that the boys would go into the business. My female cousins and I were brought up to be 'little dolls,'" another said. A third told me, "My mother had an unhappy marriage; she was ambitious, and my father just took life as it was, but still, I never thought about any other kind of life for myself except wife and mother."

I found that although most of the women whom I interviewed spoke of their mothers sympathetically—

"my mother's life was hard; she did the best she could" was an expression I heard in various versions— few felt that they had been exposed to a life pattern they wished to repeat. (I came across only two exceptions: one, the daughter of an Irish orphan who immigrated to the United States, who told me wistfully that her mother had much more courage and adventure than she, and the second, the daughter of a wealthy woman whose life seemed almost incredibly blessed by fortune.) What then, were their hopes, wishes, ambitions? What sort of lives did they plan for themselves?

Although the replies ranged from "I never thought of myself as being anything except a wife and mother" to reports from women who had thought about the professions or the arts, there seemed to be a common denominator. My observations led me to the same conclusion that Betty Friedan reached in researching *The Feminine Mystique*: Most of us, "growing up . . . had no image of our own future"—or at best, only a sort of vague, dreaming vision. "I was just going to be a glamorous person," one woman told me, putting into words what I had sensed in scores of interviews.

Of course, there were exceptions. "There were two colleges available to me," one woman told me. "Brooklyn and Hunter. I went to an orientation session at Hunter, and we were told about the 'kind of education useful for a woman.' Young and inex-perienced as I was, I knew I didn't want to be educated to be a *woman*—I wanted to be a *person*." But the overwhelming majority of women with whom I spoke seemed to me to have made almost haphazard choices about their lives: "It's too bad that one has to make decisions at eighteen that count at forty," another interviewee said. The terror of growing up, the wish to escape into the safety of home and family rather than to develop an individual identity at twenty or twenty-one seemed to cut across the twenty-year span in the ages of the women I interviewed. "You were lucky, you younger gals," a woman at the nether end of our generation told me. "I graduated from high school in the depths of the Depression. I knew I had to go to work, and when I married, we had to struggle to make ends meet. Then my husband was drafted, and I followed him from Army camp to Army camp until he went overseas." But the hard reality of the war and Depression finally did not seem to have the effect of making her life plan noticeably different from those of her somewhat younger sisters. Her job, too, was dead-end and stopgap—she was a clerk in a Wall Street bond office—and as soon as her husband was discharged, she, like the others of her generation, became a housewife.

Sorting it out, then, the determining factor in the choice the women of my generation made—a life plan based on the sexual role, rather than on the development and utilization of intelligence, energy, imagination, creativity, and education—seems to have been less a matter of individual psychology than of general sociology. The women with whom I spoke came from varying backgrounds, were taught divergent values, but the ways in which they were to find their identities as young women were remarkably similar.

The lifework we chose involved no vague, misty visions. There was no need for us to chart out our own courses; the instructions came in from all sides. The goals, methods, results we were to achieve, in short our entire *modus vivendi* was spelled out in the media, in the "serious" literature of the times.

If the first postwar years had been devoted to helping husbands through college, now the task at hand was to propel them to success in business. A spate of articles appeared in the women's magazines, explaining how industry "rated" those fiercely ambitious young "executives." "Are You Holding Your Husband Back?" the articles asked, listing "ten ways to help your husband up the ladder of success." Maintaining a perfect home was crucial, of course. (There evidently was one perfect menu for entertaining "his boss"—chicken with some gourmet touch, cream and mushrooms, perhaps, or a stuffing of ham and cheese, and an elaborate dessert based on the cake mix that was the magazine's steadiest advertiser.)

The "home" that was to be a backdrop for all this was a ranch or split-level house in the suburbs (bought with a minimum down payment and a 4½ percent GI mortgage), furnished with as much wall-to-wall carpet and as many appliances as could be afforded on "easy credit payments." Wedding checks and then paychecks were precisely earmarked for purchases of furniture—modern or Early American decor were the alternatives; there were cobbler's benches in "tavern" finish, coordinated silver and china, and Melmac dinnerware for "everyday." The house itself exorcised the demon that had haunted the children of the Depression who had grown to adulthood in this time of prosperity. "It is no coincidence that some of the most popular tract houses look like the gingerbread house in Hansel and Gretel," writes Gail Jackson Putney in *The Challenge to Women.* Our generation was "trying to live a fairy tale in which the wicked witch of poverty has been burned to a crisp. . . . [The] dream of happiness was a large mother-centered family that needed no scrimping."

The decor and appliances necessary to create the "mother-centered family" (the heart of those new suburban houses were the "eat-in kitchens" that reversed the building patterns of the past two decades during which the old-time family kitchens had shrunk to efficient, tiled laboratories) required constant upkeep and care. America entered the detergent age. The cake of Fels-Naphtha soap, box of Oxydol, and bottle of Javel water that had kept our mother's houses gleaming were replaced in ours with an endless array of "special cleansers," polishers, and waxers. Keeping house, for all the laborsaving devices we had been promised would make homemaking a joy, became increasingly complicated and increasingly time-consuming. Cake mixes and frozen preparations, instead of being "convenience foods," became the basis of "gourmet cookery." The idea was not to save time, but to produce more "exciting and imaginative meals." Dutifully, we spent endless hours at the supermarket, selecting those items that would make our homemaking, cooking, entertaining perfect—involving ourselves in the never-ending pursuit of a domestic paradise.

The women with whom I spoke bear out my memory that in my choice of domesticity above all other options, I did very little soul-searching at the time. Did we think longingly of the "outside" world? Did it occur to us that we had embarked on a lifework that would, of necessity, end in the not-too-distant future? The answer I got was overwhelmingly no.

Part of the reason for our lack of questioning was, as Betty Friedan points out, the constant "sexual sell" that industry used in its efforts to expand its consumer market in order to fill the void left by the end of defense and war production. We were manipulated by motivational researchers and advertising agencies (remember the best seller of the day, *The Hucksters?*) into believing we could be given "the sense of identity, purpose, creativity, the self-realization, even sexual joy . . . by the buying of things." The sexual sell was reinforced, of course, by the interpretation of the psychiatric theories of the day—since anatomy was destiny, the woman whose horizons were larger than the boundaries of her own home was psychologically monstrous. A plethora of marriage manuals, books on psychology, tomes by family counselors and sociologists "proved" that the truly fulfilled woman, in the words of Dr. Marynia Farnham and Ferdinand Lundberg (authors of the most popular of all those "back to anatomy" books, *Modern Woman: The Lost Sex*), directed her creative outlets toward "activity inward"—in a word, childbearing and rearing.

The perfect home and, even as it would later turn out, to some extent the husband became only props—part of the stage setting for what was our major lifework: the bearing and rearing of children. Before we were individuals or even wives, we were mothers.

The two-child family of the Depression years was obsolete; mothering became both qualitatively and quantitatively different from what it had been since the turn of the century. According to Dr. Jesse Bernard in *The Future of Marriage*:

. . . between 1947 and 1957, the decade of the
so-called feminine mystique or marital togetherness,
all of a sudden . . . the statistical curves began to
change their direction. . . . The birthrate, which,
with fluctuations due to wars and depressions had
been declining for as long as records had been kept,
. . . did not resume the longtime downward trend
after the expected postwar spurt. It even . . .
remained high until late in the 1950's. Nor were
these simply delayed or anticipated babies. They
were additional babies—third, fourth, fifth and
sixth. . . .

Interviewing women about the years in which they
were primarily mothers, I asked them what they recall
of their feelings. Did they find "mothering" satisfying,
fulfilling? Did they feel that they had made the right
choice in selecting motherhood as their primary source
of endeavor?

The answers are strangely at variance with what the
books and media were telling us at the time. Looking
backward, most women no longer see motherhood as a
holy calling—which is not to say that most of them
regret having had families. What they do seem to
regret is the fact that they made mothering the whole
focus of their lives. "It seems to be that I was
exhausted all the time," was the response that I got
most frequently. "I just took it for granted that since I
had the children, I had to do everything for them. I
was afraid of failing as a mother, and I wore myself
ragged." "I was overconscientious" was another
often-repeated response. "I didn't question *why* I was
doing what I was doing—my only questions were
self-doubts about my ability to be a good mother."
And, most directly, from the mother of five: "I used to

lose my temper a lot and yell at the children. I prayed every night for God to help me be a better mother."

The guilt was heavily reinforced for us by the idealized image of motherhood that in these years of the seventies seems almost a mass psychosis. Motherhood was supposed to be intrinsically fulfilling. Even childbirth itself was supposed to have been a treat. There was something declasse about admitting that labor was painful. "Natural childbirth" was the *sine qua non* of the truly womanly woman. Dr. Grantly Dick-Read's book on childbirth without drugs became a best seller; women who opted for saddle block or other anesthesia were somehow copping out. Breast-feeding, too, was promoted not only as "natural" (as surely it is) but as necessary. Mary McCarthy's wry description in *The Group* of Priss' despair at the wails of her colicky, underfed baby—"For herself, she felt sad and beaten, as though she had lost her reason for living if she could not nurse Stephen,"—brings back vivid memories of the cult of mother's milk.

But while there were still permissible outs for the dictates to rejoice in the natural functions of childbirth and breast-feeding—there were, after all, women whose pelvic indices were too narrow for labor, and one could excuse oneself for a Caesarian if it were to save one's life—there were *none* for anything less than blind devotion to the drudgeries of childbearing. In actuality, far from being a fulfillment of one's sexuality, as the psychiatric theory of the time would have us believe, motherhood was an escape from it, for imposed on the bearing and rearing of children was the puritan work ethic. In choosing motherhood, women substituted hard work for rapture; one had to be a "good" mother which meant, according to

Department of Labor statistics, something like eighty hours of work a week, a preoccupation with one's children's welfare that drained both physical and emotional energy completely, leaving no room for intellectual, sexual, or social fulfillment.

What was it that we believed we needed to *do* for our children? First, of course, there was the physical care of them. Just as the "sexual sell" had placed rigid standards on perfect housekeeping—the television commercials led us to believe that being known for having "the cleanest wash in town" was the most important accolade to which a woman could aspire—it determined the way in which children were to be fed, clothed, and cared for. What was the purpose of having an automatic washer-dryer and several shelves of special detergents if not to keep in constant use? My mother's housekeeping was above reproach, and washday—a regular event every Monday morning— was a ritual involving steaming vats of boiled starch, a washboard used as auxiliary to the wringer washing machine, bleach, blueing, clotheslines, and baskets of clothespins. But it was *once a week*; my own washer-dryer combination ran at least *twice a day* while my children were small. I was compelled, along with all the other women in my neighborhood, to change children's pajamas daily, to snatch barely soiled shirts and overalls off their protesting bodies every few hours.

Physical safety also meant a constant surveillance of children's play hours. The rush to the suburbs—"Living in the city isn't good for the children, they need their own backyards"—didn't lighten mothers' supervisory tasks. Those treelined suburban streets soon filled with traffic; the backyards fitted out with swings and jungle gyms presented their own hazards.

But the qualitative difference in motherhood that the postwar years brought was more than a matter of heightened concern about children's well-being. Motherhood had become a vocational calling, and as such, it involved status, power, tangible results. Having renounced all goals other than motherhood, women had no other fields in which to prove themselves and their worth; one gained one's laurels from one's children's progress.

To that end, women began to move back into areas of child development that the twenties and thirties had decreed the bailiwick of experts. If the trend up until then had been to increase professionalism in the schools, it now was understood that the schools and the parents were involved in a "partnership." The scope of Parent-Teacher Associations increased; the meetings were no longer, as they had been during my childhood, comfortable coffee klatches where mothers planned class picnics and raised funds for farewell presents for retiring teachers. Parents' associations moved into curricula, administration. Community groups, rather than school administrators and educators, had their say not only in such knotty problems as transportation, but also in the selection of books and material, in classroom management itself.

Nor was what had once been the province of children themselves—the management of their play activities—any longer trusted to youngsters. Play activities were tightly organized; sandlot baseball was replaced with Little League, requiring parents to appear religiously at all games, to raise funds for uniforms, to organize parties to celebrate victories or mourn defeats. A youngster's entrance into the Girl or Boy Scouts provided nearly a full-time job for his parents; there were positions to be filled—Den Mother and *Assistant* Den Mother. (I remember spending an entire evening as apprentice Den Mother, receiving instructions on how to conduct a proper flag-salute ceremony.) Added to all this were the extracurricular activities mothers were to perform on their own. Children needed dancing lessons, music lessons, religious instruction, not to mention necessities such as dental and orthodontial care, all involving strict scheduling and chauffeuring—and constant maternal participation.

Our children were to be perfect; to what other ends had we renounced all other interests, activities, goals? As they grew up, instead of lightening, the pressures of motherhood increased. Whereas earlier generations had seen full-time mothering as an occupation required for the first seven or eight years of each child's life, we extended the scope until late adolescence. "I thought my children would need me less as they grew up," I used to hear women say, "but when they reach teen age, that's when they really need me!" Those "needs" involved undiminished physical care and increased "guidance" and "direction." The pressure for academic excellence increased. As the war-crop babies reached college age, competition for college entrance reached almost hysterical proportions. Junior high school students were warned about possibilities of rejection from the "college of their choice"; mother was needed to prod, to assist with homework assignments, to provide remedial and tutorial services.

As we had been warned by the media and social scientists of the dangers of losing our femininity by "competing with men," so we were now warned of the dangers of haphazard motherhood. But perhaps all the buttressing we received as justification for our full-time roles as mothers, from psychologists, sociologists, educators—all the "experts" upon whose testimony and theory we depended so heavily and accepted so completely—was almost superfluous. We needed less prodding, perhaps, from the outside than we got, for our own needs were compelling enough to ensure that we would carry out the job to our fullest capacities. Our needs for love, work, knowledge—the drives upon whose satisfaction human happiness is predicated—were *all* directed toward "activity inward." In a word, we put all our eggs in one basket, and we left ourselves no other course of action but to derive all our satisfactions from motherhood.

Sublimating our needs for knowledge, we turned our backs on the larger world. The McCarthy period, with its "know-nothing" mood, passed, barely noticed. While bitter battles were fought by educators, writers, actors against blacklisting, political repression, American women retreated behind the safe barrier of preoccupation with their own domestic concerns. "I didn't even have time to read the newspaper," women told me, commenting on their abdication from citizenship duties. Whereas forty years earlier women's organizations worked fervently on issues such as poverty (the settlement movement, for example), birth control, labor law, founding hospitals, and expanding education, volunteer groups in the fifties narrowed their horizons to personal domestic concerns. Perhaps this retreat was a general

reaction engendered by the atom bomb, by the
confusion America was experiencing in the face of the
changing world situation—the defeat of Chiang, the
rise of the socialist countries climaxing in the startling
advances of the Soviet Union in the space race—but, at
any rate, as Betty Friedan illustrates by quoting the
editor of "a large woman's magazine," American
women were "not interested in the broad public issues
of the day . . . in national or international affairs . . .
in politics, unless it's related to an immediate need in
the home. You just can't write about ideas or broad
issues of the day for women. That's why we're
publishing 90 percent service now and 10 percent
general interest."

If our needs for love were channeled into preoccupation with children, our needs for work and
achievement directed toward the maintenance of our
homes, what about all those other yearnings, desires—
recognition, challenge, adventure, power? Sorting
through the answers I got to my questions, I sensed
that somehow they were simply turned away, held in
abeyance. The pattern was simply to find expression in
self-renunciation, and I heard it a hundred ways. "If
the children weren't having problems in school or
with their friends, if my husband seemed happy and
doing well in his job, then I felt satisfied." Some
women spoke about feeling "guilty" when they failed
to find completion in their devotion to their families.
"I felt selfish when I thought about myself. I thought I
had trouble 'giving,' and when I looked around, I saw
other women doing so much more for their families
than I did." And a recurring theme was this one:
"Sometimes when I became dissatisfied and restless, I
would tell myself that I couldn't take time for what I

wanted now, but that someday the children would be grown, and I would be able to do all the things I wanted to."

What all those vague "things" we were to do, when suddenly our roles were to come abruptly and irreversibly to an end, was never spelled out for us, never seemed to merit serious attention from the psychologists, sociologists, or educators who so strongly reinforced our selection of the "womanly role." Nor indeed, were we ever given any hints that after a lifetime spent in deferring our needs and wishes to the service of others, we were not properly equipped to take upon ourselves the privilege and responsibility for our own self-expression.

Toward the end of the era, Betty Friedan wrote:

> The fact remains that the girl who wastes her college years without acquiring serious interests, and wastes her early years marking time until she finds a man gambles with the possibilities of an identity of her own. . . . It is not that easy for a woman who has defined herself wholly as wife and mother for ten or fifteen years to find a new identity at thirty-five or forty or fifty.

But the warning was never given to us. Facing the "jumping-off point" in our middle years, we were to find ourselves, for the first time in our lives, on our own—with no clues to the uncertain future.

Chapter 4

THE DISPOSABLE WOMAN

And then, when things have been going along in a known and established fashion for perhaps 15 or 20 years, the entire lovely creation begins to show signs of impermanence and of still another transition still to come. She has had her children earlier and closer together than her grandmother did, bearing her last child when she is twenty-six . . . somewhere between thirty-five and forty . . . they are adolescents, away from home much of the day and becoming highly independent. The nest is not empty yet, but . . . it has an ominously empty look . . . her husband is busier than ever with his work . . . he rarely needs her encouragement and advice. . . . All in all, she is close to being out of a job and to losing her carefully built up sense of self . . . she thrashes around uncertainly in search of new goals, new roles, a new identity . . . she is that curious phenomenon, a thirty-five to forty year old adolescent.

—MORTON HUNT, *Her Infinite Variety*

We are told we are the luckiest women in the world, we 21,000,000 American women between the ages of forty-one and sixty. The great majority of us are married, living in "nuclear families"—households composed of a husband and wife and possibly children still at home. We are affluent, healthy, better looking, better dressed, and more youthful than our mothers ever dreamed of being at our age. We are heiresses to all the medical advances and technological miracles of our time. We have the gift of life itself, for at forty we have an average life expectancy of nearly as many more years as we have already lived—more than a quarter of a century more years than our grandmothers might have expected and nearly a decade more than our brothers and husbands can look forward to.

We have, then, in a word *everything.*

And yet there is a curious contradiction in this view. Told that we are the envy of the world, we are denied permission to a real appraisal of our situations. The magnitude of the crises of middle age is diminished for us. "What have *you* got to complain about?" we are asked, and we chide ourselves for being ungrateful, for our "self-pity." As we were expected to be "fulfilled" as young women in our roles as wives and mothers— any difficulties we may have experienced then were evidence of a denial of our "femininity"—we are expected to be serene in our middle years. The word "neurotic" is the unspoken part of the appellation "middle-aged woman."

But the crisis of middle age is real, no aberration, part of the human condition. In German-speaking countries, the panic of encroaching middle age is called *Torschluss,* a closing of the gates on youth. In his brilliant and poetic essay "The Stages of Life," Carl Jung writes about the profundity of the conflicts that come with the "psyche's development through youth and middle age."

> . . . I must take for comparison the daily course of the sun—but a sun that is endowed with human feeling and man's limited consciousness. In the morning it rises from the nocturnal sea of unconsciousness and looks upon the wide, bright world . . . in an expanse that steadily widens the higher it climbs in the firmament . . . the sun will discover its significance; it will see the attainment of the greatest possible dissemination of its blessings. . . . At the

stroke of noon the descent begins. And the descent means the reversal of all the ideals and values that were cherished in the morning. The sun falls into contradiction with itself. It is as though it should draw in its rays instead of emitting them.

What, then, is happening to us during the rise and descent of our own suns? Jung contends that we sought the "solution of the problems of youth by restricting ourselves to the attainable," a process that "is only temporarily valid and not lasting in a deeper sense." We adapted our own natures to conform, to gain success. As we "struggle, suffer and win victories with the ideals . . . which in the period of youth lead us out into life . . . they grow together with our own being." We then "apparently change into them, we seek to perpetuate them indefinitely." The crisis comes when as "we approach the middle of life . . . the better we have succeeded . . . the more it appears as if we had discovered the right course and the right ideals and principles of behavior. For this reason we suppose them to be eternally valid, and make it a virtue of unchangeably clinging to them. We overlook the essential fact that the social goal is attained only at the cost of diminuation of personality."

What is the result of this clinging to earlier goals and methods? Jung continues:

> Statistics show a rise in the frequency of mental depressions in men about forty. In women the neurotic difficulties begin somewhat earlier. We see that in this phase of life—between thirty-five and forty—an important change in the human psyche is in preparation. Often it is something like a slow change in a person's character; in another certain

traits may come to light which had disappeared
since childhood; or again, one's previous inclinations and interests begin to weaken and others take
their place. . . .

The worst of it all is that intelligent and cultivated
people live all their lives without even knowing of
the possibility of such transformations. Wholly
unprepared, they embark on the second half of life
. . . worse still, we take this step with the false
assumption that our truths and ideals will serve us
as hitherto. But we cannot live in the afternoon of
life according to the program of life's morning; for
what was great in the morning will be little at
evening, and what in the morning was true will at
evening become a lie.

The first crisis of middle age, then, is within the
psyche itself, as the values and aspirations of youth
come up for examination in the light of the experiences
and knowledge which we have gained through living.
As in adolescence, there is a sifting through the
standards imposed by society, by family and friends,
and a striking out in an attempt to find the parts of the
self that were repressed or neglected during the years
in which we strove for tangible achievement.

But the crises of middle age go beyond the
metaphysical level; superimposed on the changes
within the psyche itself are the reality problems of our
daily lives. There are the somewhat abrupt changes in
our bodies—or what we perceive to be changes—the
situations we find ourselves in with regard to
adolescent and adult children; to husbands, who, too,
are facing a jumping-off point; to aging parents or to
the loss of them; to the loss of friends and the difficulty
of replacing them; to vocational and financial realities;

to unexpected and unplanned-for leisure time—in short, for the termination of one role and the need to substitute another. Our conflicts, then, are both internal and external.

To begin with, what is happening to *us?* We have reached a milestone—our fortieth birthdays—the point of the "great divide." However gradually the signs of aging have appeared, it now seems we have gone irrevocably "over the hill." Jack Benny remained perpetually at thirty-nine; the symbolic difference between one's thirty-ninth and fortieth birthdays are light-years apart. The small signs that we have felt until now were reversible—"laugh lines" and crow's feet, stretch marks, gray hair—no longer seem responsive to our efforts with moisturizer and cocoa butter, tint and foundation creams. There is no longer the belief that a good night's sleep will erase the circles under our eyes; they are here to stay and, worse, will grow more pronounced each day. We are caught in the dilemma of trying to find appropriate clothes—some middle way between the matronly outfits that mean surrender and the youthful modes that we see (with a sinking sensation in the pits of our stomachs) succeed only in making us look older.

We observe physiological changes despite the knowledge that we are still at an age when we can expect vigorous health. Our eye muscles have weakened; the term "presbyopia" strikes a blow at our hearts—it means "old eyes," and it confers upon us the symbol of aging, the ubiquitous reading glasses. We are encouraged by our physicians to come more frequently for physical checkups; we know, with a sense of dread, that we are entering the age in which we will be watching, with increasing vigilance,

for signs of high blood pressure, gallbladder disturb-
ances, respiratory problems. We are told, now, to have
Pap smears twice a year instead of once; the specter of
menopause hangs over us, and we half listen to the old
wives' tales about its perils. If we are heavy smokers,
we experience the ill effects of the habit: We hear our
voices thickening; we listen to the pounding of our
hearts with the palpitations of tachycardia. If we were
headache-prone, we are now at the age in which
migraine attacks reach their peak. If we have had
digestive difficulties in the past—and even if we
haven't—there are suddenly a host of foods that "don't
agree with us": We pick the onion out of our salads;
we order Sanka when we go out to dinner. We worry
about not getting enough sleep; our bodies are no
longer resilient enough to take the abuse that we
unthinkingly gave them in our youth. At a time when
we need *all* our resources, we notice, regretfully, that
the blithe good health we have taken for granted is no
longer something upon which we can depend, and
sometimes, grudgingly, we must make accommodations.

At the same time that we look inward with a sense of
foreboding, we become conscious of what is happening to those around us, first, probably, to our
husbands. In the jargon of the professionals, they are
entering the "mid-life crisis." Dr. Herbert Klemme,
director of the Division of Industrial Mental Health at
the Menninger Foundation, who conducts intensive
weekly behavior seminars for male executives and
physicians (and recently, for women, too), lists some
of the symptoms of what he calls "the death of young
loves and dreams: divorce, alcoholism, depression
masked as chronic fatigue, impotence, loss of zest and

energy, and a high susceptibility to colds." Continuing the explanation, Dr. Klemme adds, "Our work ethic provides an ideal cover for the executive who avoids looking at himself, at his inner life, by taking on more work—although he may complain about depleted energies." For the blue-collar worker, Dr. Klemme continues, the symptoms are masked in an increased reliance on recreation—perhaps drinking or gambling, but in either case, the evidence of stress is there.

While menopause in women is a definite physiological change, the area of male menopause remains cloudy. Women's "stages" are clearly marked by the beginning and cessation of menstruation; for men the signs are subtle, measurable less dramatically, only by the increase and decrease of sexual potency. But whether or not there is a male equivalent to female menopause is nearly irrelevant. "So much of what a person feels is emotional is what society expects from people," according to Dr. Michael M. Baden, deputy chief medical examiner of New York City.

What is happening to men in one way corresponds to what we as women are experiencing; in another, it is directly opposed. On the purely physical level, there are similarities in the signs of encroaching age, facial and bodily aging. Although society inculcates in us the totally erroneous idea that men age more attractively than women do, the loss of youth and beauty is a cruel blow to both sexes. A forty-seven-year-old New York advertising executive's rueful description of his impact on the opposite sex is instantly recognizable: "There is a chemistry between men and women . . . that takes place when you see a pretty girl on the street. Then one day you walk past her and you still feel it, but she looks through you as if you were a pane of glass."

However distressing these changes are, they are frivolous compared to the health problems of aging men. While women in the middle years are prey to a variety of ailments that range from minor to major, their longevity statistics are reassuring; men's concern about their survival through this period is sustained by the most ominous statistics. The middle-aged man is the nation's number one target for cardiovascular diseases and cancer. Not all the cholesterol watching, jogging, cutting back on liquor and cigarettes can really convince the forty-five-year-old man that he will be spared; his vulnerability is brought home to him each time he sees a friend or acquaintance of his age succumb.

Beyond the physical, though are the vocational and sociological stresses. The middle years represent the peak of men's achievement in business and professions. Charting the careers of the men who were involved in this study (as seen and reported by their wives), I found virtually no surprises. Each had gone through the hard years of striving in his twenties and thirties; for all the propaganda about family values, nearly all the women with whom I spoke told me that they thought their husbands had placed first priority on their work. Then, in the forties, when men approach the zenith of their careers, there is a paradox, for the closer they come toward the culmination of their ambitions, the greater the sense of insecurity. As Dr. Baden explains:

> . . . in the man's occupational world, emphasis is on the young and "coming" so that a man of forty

may be looking anxiously over his shoulder at the wolf pack yapping and slobbering at his heels as he slips along over competitive business ice. At forty, the status of many a man, either in business or on the assembly line is frozen, so he feels stuck and fearful.

How does this pattern of male achievement manifest itself in the lives of women? Interviewing women, I asked these questions: How do you view your husband's career at this time? Does he seem satisfied with his work? Does he spend more or less time on the job than he did ten or so years ago? Does he seem more or less preoccupied with his work when he is at home? Do you share his work interests to a greater or lesser degree now? Are *you* satisfied with his achievement, worried about his future? And most directly, I asked, how does your husband's career now affect your marriage and your relationship to him? Where are *you* in this picture?

Interestingly, although most of the women whom I interviewed were proud of their husbands' achievements, there were few who did not speak of their own resentments and dissatisfactions and none who were not concerned because the places their husbands were in to a large extent determined their own. Nearly all told me that they thought their husbands were working harder and siphoning *more* emotional and physical energy into their work than they had as young men. "Every rung up the ladder means more responsibility," one woman told me. "He not only brings work home with him, he's on call all the time." Wives of professional men, doctors and lawyers, were particularly vocal. "It takes twenty years to build a good law practice," one complained, "but now that he has it, it consumes all his time. The cases have gotten 'so big' he can't turn them over to his assistant." "It took him fifteen years to complete his training," the wife of a psychiatrist told me. "He feels he has to make up for lost time. He sees patients six days a week and only takes one night off."

A second pattern that emerged was that the women felt less involved in their husband's work than they had during the "building years." "When he opened his first luncheonette," the wife of a restaurateur told me, "I helped him pick out the floor covering, I went with him when he had the sign printed to select the style; he even told me how much bread he ordered the first day. Now, sometimes weeks go by and we don't talk about the business; I couldn't imagine his asking me for my opinion about it. As far as I'm concerned, the business is *his* baby; I just take it for granted." Some of the women spoke frankly of their boredom: "He used to tell me about office politics; but I didn't know the people, and I tuned out when he talked about it." One was particularly honest in her appraisal of her own role: "When he used to talk about his job, I would get panicky, and I guess after a while he wanted to spare me the worry. Now I just assume everything is all right; he doesn't talk shop at home." A number of them were resentful: "When the children were little, I didn't have time. Now I would *like* to talk about the business, but he never tells me anything." And several excused the lack of communication this way: "He's tired when he comes home, and he wants to just forget about the job. We don't talk about it at all."

The women whose life experiences are the subject of this book were all, as I have explained, middle-class rather than working-class women. They were, by and large, married to "successful" men, the group that Dr. Klemme explains, is most likely to take out their tensions in the work ethic. Many women sensed their husband's tensions, even without directly discussing them with the men. "I know when he has business troubles," a number of women indicated to me. "He gets silent, drinks more." Many women told me about physical tension and psychosomatic ailments. "His chest is like a clenched fist," one woman said graphically. "No wonder he's always complaining about chest pains and going for cardiographs." Although several women had experienced the results of their husband's worst fears being realized, only one spoke directly to me about it. Her husband, a fifty-five-year-old advertising executive, had suddenly lost his job and was unable to find another. "You always know that there's somebody gunning for your job," she told me, "but when the ax falls, somehow you're unprepared. We both went into a depression; we didn't go anywhere or see anyone, and of course our sex life died. Now he's on his feet again; but his ego took a terrible beating, and he's still not himself."

It is this question of male ego, as much as the practical concerns of income and security, at a time when perhaps there are the greatest needs for high income—children in college, increased medical costs—that figured in the women's thinking. Some women spoke openly about their worries, and the gist of what they had to say was something like this: "He's worried that he's getting older, losing his energy and strength; he worries about the younger rat pack crowding in on him; I'm afraid that he turns for reassurance to younger women."

What the women spoke of, then, was the fact that

they were recipients of two kinds of tensions: the vocational ones and the anxieties that their husband's desire to make some kind of achievement in worldly terms may prompt drastic changes in life-style—that the middle years are the time for the final fling, for extramarital affairs or remarriage. At a time when they had hoped to find their marriages solidified, they felt insecure; in the years in which they found that their domestic duties were lightened enough to provide time and energy for their husbands, their husbands were preoccupied with work; that, in fact the life-styles of husbands and wives during the twenty years before middle-age seemed to take them not to the same place, finally, but into separate worlds.

If, then, what I heard married women express was a feeling of isolation, what is the lot of single women, particularly those who had never been married? Among the women with whom I spoke there were only a few in this category—a fact in accordance with our general statistical patterns: About 95 percent of the women of my generation have been married at some time in their lives. For this minority, however, there were certain pressures and tensions unique to them and others which they seemed to share with married women.

The regrets about the loss of youth and beauty seemed to me to be widely felt; if married women were haunted by the fear that they were in jeopardy of losing their men to younger women, single women were particularly aware of the passing years for other reasons. My feeling was that since each of the single women I interviewed had always been in the business or professional world, she was more conscious of her appearance than most married women. Aging meant more than a lack of allure for men, though. It also meant, to some, a business handicap. "When the firm I worked for went under last year," a successful designer told me, "I found myself in competition with much younger women for jobs. I realized that my experience wasn't so much an asset anymore, it was a problem. Besides the fact that a lot of employers like having young women around, my age meant that I was 'heavy' for some jobs; there were a lot of young designers around who would work for much less than I would."

Perhaps the most difficult pressure upon unmarried women in the middle years, though, is the adjustment to the knowledge that there is no longer the possibility of having children. Even among women who are least ambivalent about not marrying—"I never really felt that I wanted to give up my independence"—the acceptance of permanent childlessness was difficult. A friend from my college years, a teacher whose life had been spent in devotion to her job, travel, and a love affair with the outdoors, expressed it this way: "I've always had the feeling that I might marry sometime, and a couple of times I've come very close. But I somehow felt I had time; there was no real pressure on me. Now I realize that what I've given up is a family—and I've always loved children. I suppose if I married now, I could adopt an older child, or I might marry a man with children, but it isn't the same thing. I'm not so sure I made a mistake in not marrying, but I'm forty-six, and I'll never have a child of my own—and that's painful."

The whole question of women's relationships to their children at this time in life concerned me particularly. As a divorcée, I wondered what my life would be in the next few years as my younger son, following his older brother, went off to college. My position, statistically, is not average; most women in their early forties are living in nuclear homes with a husband and at least one child still at home. Their youngest children have entered adolescence; the oldest have reached the age that is called young adult. Were other women as preoccupied as I with their relationships now to their children? I wondered.

Phrasing the questions, I tried to find the continuing patterns in motherhood. Do you feel that your children require more or less of you? I asked now. At what stage in their lives did you feel most useful and fulfilled? When did you feel least? Do you feel you have been successful as a mother? How have you succeeded or failed? What has been your relationship with your children during the years of their growing up, and what it is now? How do you envision it in the future?

What is the role of motherhood, then, in the life of a woman who has reached forty? In a word, *ambiguous.* Although some of the women with whom I spoke told me they "enjoyed" their children more as they went from adolescence toward young adulthood, a clear majority thought that this was the least satisfying and most anxiety-provoking stage of motherhood. A surprising number expressed the idea that they felt less confidence in their children and less in themselves as mothers at this time than at any other.

"I began to have trouble with my daughter when she was about thirteen," a forty-eight-year-old housewife told me, describing attitudes and experiences that I was to find fairly common. "She began to challenge my authority, not just small things, where I could give in, but about issues that I was *not* prepared to let go on—hitchhiking, for instance." Others spoke about the "moods" of adolescence and their difficulty in dealing with them. "I watch him mope around the house and lock himself in his room for days on end with the record player blasting. I know that he's got troubles of his own with his friends, or his love life, but when I see that surly expression on his face, I lose patience." The alternating challenge to parental authority and the increased demands for attention and service were a frequent source of difficulty. "Everybody around here wants me to do everything for them," another woman, a sculptor and the mother of three, complained. "The only thing is they also want me to be *invisible*."

The blurred outlines of the role as mother of adolescents was often mentioned. "Teen-agers don't know whether they're children or adults," I was told. "One minute my daughter is a four-year-old, and then suddenly she startles me with her maturity and sense." Many spoke about the difficulties of maintaining a consistent set of standards at home, under the barrage of outside "peer group" pressure. "'All the kids are doing it!' is the answer to any rule I try to lay down," one woman explained. "I really think that I have very little influence over my children at this time. I used to think that they let their hair grow and refused to shave as a way of rebelling against us—it drove my husband nearly crazy when the boys came down to dinner in T-shirts—but now I realize that isn't so. They don't care much what *we* think—they do things to be part of the crowd out there. It's their friends' opinions they care about; we're irrelevant." Many women spoke anxiously about their children as part of the "drug culture." "How can you get around it?" I was asked. "All the kids use it."

A great many women seemed to feel that sociological factors rather than the natural stages of life were responsible for the difficulties they were experiencing with their children. Here is a statement that I heard in one form or another from several women: "My children are fundamentally good kids, but the trouble with them is that everything has come too easy. They've never had to work for what they get, and they figure the world owes them a living. When I was a girl, I didn't ask my parents for anything. It was during the Depression, and they had enough trouble making ends meet. I knew that if I wanted clothes or anything special, I had to go out and work. I had a lot of respect for my parents. I knew they were doing the best they could. If I don't give my kids everything, they think they're being deprived, and they resent me."

Several women spoke of their anger at their children's rejections of their values. "My daughter is a radical," a well-to-do housewife complained. "She makes fun of our possessions; she tells me I'm middle-class; she sneers at the way we live. But I notice that she doesn't miss a chance to get all the goodies she can. When I went to Florida last winter, she was perfectly content to spend her whole winter vacation from college lying around the patio. I asked her why she didn't spend a couple of weeks with the migrant workers, and she wouldn't talk to me."

But conversely, other women thought that part of the difficulties they were encountering had to do with the obstacles society placed in the way of their children: "I feel sorry for my kids in a way. I don't think they're a lucky generation at all, even though they have a lot of material things. They've been kept babies much too long, maybe because we didn't have anything much else to do but be mothers. They were deprived of their independence because we had to be perfect parents. Sometimes I think the best thing adolescents can have is some good healthy neglect, so they can find themselves, and they get very little of that. Somebody is always sitting on them to make sure they do well in school, so that they can get into college. Everybody is suspicious of them—do they take drugs, experiment with sex? I still have to drive my sixteen-year-old son to the movies; when I was a kid, I lived in the city, I could take a bus. Here, there's no way for them to get around by themselves, there's too much danger—of being mugged or attacked—there are too many rules. They can't go to most movies; the movies are rated R or X, and they can't get in. It's hard on parents, and it's hard on the kids."

Another theme that emerged was that of family conflicts centering on the changing roles of children and parents. "I have to stand between my son and his father all the time," one woman told me. "His father is always telling him to take a bath or making remarks about his long-haired friends. When the children were little, we more or less saw eye to eye on the children, or at least I was the one who was responsible and made the decisions. Now suddenly my husband is taking notice, and he's critical of the children and of me." Other women described the classic difficulties that emerged when their daughters began to date. "He sees every boy that comes to the house as a potential rapist. I told him he has to have faith in his children, but he tells me he remembers when he was young and how he was always trying to make out with girls. He tells me I don't understand what those boys are really like."

Some of the women spoke about the difficulties in

living arrangements as the children matured: "I used to be able to put them to bed by nine o'clock, and then the evening was ours. Now they're up until all hours. I have no privacy, and when we go to bed, I can't even have sex; I can hear them walking back and forth in the hall to the bathroom." And then, of course, there were a host of minor complaints: the telephone; the family car; the children's sloppiness and unwillingness to share in household tasks.

Most women drew distinctions between the aspects of the roles as mothers. For example, nearly all of them spoke of the arduous work of rearing a child from infancy through childhood. But while the early years were marked by concern for the children's physical well-being, most women thought that the *emotional demands* that were made on them during their children's adolescence were more trying. Some of them described a feeling of helplessness about the role that they had not experienced in earlier years. "It's hard for me to let go," one said frankly, and while others spoke with relief about the fact that their children spent more time away from the family as they grew older, most of them expressed uneasiness at the prospect of facing changes in the family relationships that were an inevitable part of their children's growing up. One woman whom I interviewed was, in fact, in the throes of a major crisis: Her younger daughter's departure for college had brought her up against the knowledge that she and her husband had built their marriage around their positions as mother and father. With the children gone, they discovered they had little in common and nothing to talk about.

Interviewing women at this crucial stage in their lives, I sensed that their satisfaction in life had much to do with how they viewed the results of their years as mothers. The women who had spoken about their lives as young women in these terms, "At night, when I went to bed, I would think about my husband and children; if they had been happy that day, I was happy," shifted their emphasis in talking about their lives after forty. I heard something like this from many of them: "If my children are turning out well, I am happy. If they do not give me that promise, I view my life as a failure." The middle years are the time when either the chips are in or the handwriting is on the wall. There is no longer the dailiness of the job at hand, and one's happiness and sense of achievement are now predicated on factors over which one has little control. The women whose children had developed in ways that brought status and reassurance to them— were doing well at school or in careers, had made appropriate and satisfactory personal relationships— showed a measure of contentment, while those whose children deviated from parental expectations were unhappy. I think particularly of a friend who had returned to college, taken a degree, and found a career for herself as a librarian while her children were of school age. Describing her life currently—she is fifty—she told me, "The two years that my son was a dropout were the worst in my life. Now that he is back to college and doing well, I feel I am finding myself." Her own career achievements, then, gave her little satisfaction at the time that her role as a mother was under a cloud; despite her other accomplishments and interests, her sense of worth was unalterably inter-twined with her children's success.

The habit of renunciation of selfhood and the pattern of living one's life through others seemed constantly to emerge as the barrier to happiness among women reaching forty. "My family, my husband, my children no longer need me," or perhaps, "no longer need me in ways that I find familiar and acceptable and have experience and guidelines to follow," seemed to be the sometimes unspoken message in what women told me. Sometimes the statement was modified to include a sense of relief at the lightening of responsibility: "With the children off and on their own, I have time for the things *I* want to do." But at best, the new freedom was a mixed blessing, carrying with it the demands for self-determination and direction.

The crumbling of familiar patterns extended into areas beyond relationships in the nuclear family. It was not just that women were up against the knowledge that they were no longer the hub of the home; their place in the larger scheme of things had drastically altered with the approach of their fortieth birthdays. For example, many had moved, or were moving, from the middle generation—children to their parents, as well as parents to their children—into the older generation. The death, illness, or mental incompetency of mothers and fathers increasingly becomes a factor in one's life after the fourth decade—a crisis of middle age that I was to hear expressed in a number of ways.

At its most basic root, the death or disintegration of one's parents is a harsh reminder of one's own mortality. "I haven't recovered from the shock of seeing how my father has aged." The experience had a particular poignancy for the woman who told me that she had left her home in Czechoslovakia at nineteen, a few weeks before the Soviet invasion. Her mother had died; her father, whom she last saw in the full vigor of his prime, was now, twenty-four years later, unmistakably an old man. But the same knowledge came more subtly to other women; seeing one's parents reaching the end of their lives or dying, particularly in a society that does not provide the extended family for comfort and security during times of loss, constitutes another of the crises of middle age for which we have had little or no preparation.

The changes that are taking place within our own family patterns are the most significant ones, but they are only a part of the shifting scene that is an inevitable part of our lives during the middle years. We live in a peripatetic society; the average American family changes residence every four years. Our children go to college half a continent or more away; they settle down, not in our towns or even states, but possibly thousands of miles away. Among the women whom I interviewed there were some whose immediate families were scattered all over the world: a son and daughter-in-law and a grandchild she had never seen in South America; a second son on a Fulbright scholarship in Sweden. Another woman's Christmas plans one year included four trips to the airport to claim her visiting relatives. Neighborhoods "turn over"; neighbors of twenty years retire, go South to live; suddenly one is surrounded by strangers. Watching the moving van arrive to transport the belongings of my neighbors to a small apartment in the city—their children were grown; they no longer needed four bedrooms and a half acre of lawn—I thought of the not-too-distant past when our boys had shot baskets into the hoop over my garage door while I cooked dinner, and I wept in anticipation of the loneliness I knew I faced.

Jules Henry, in a perceptive essay called "The Forty-Year Jitters in Married Urban Women," puts his finger on the "middle class intangibles" that are part of a society "committed to evanescence." These includes "upward and downward mobility—people's financial situations change, bring about a breaking off of old community and the substitution of new friends and acquaintances." There is the "peripatetic nature of our living patterns. . . . Thus in our culture," Dr. Henry continues, "there is no guarantee that we will never be alone . . . the phone may stop . . . people die." Circumstances of life separate us from those who have spelled security for us in the past; our lives and theirs take us into different directions. "The ills that life brings are easier to bear when we are not so alone," Dr. Henry concludes. "Women have so few people they can rely on that when the phantasms of aging begin to gather, they must fight them alone without an extended or protecting community."

To deal constructively with the built-in problems of the middle years, to cope with a society that offers us so little in the way of sustaining comfort, to find purpose and pleasure in our lives as the "phantasms of aging" draw closer is no easy challenge. To do it, we need not only to appraise the forces that have shaped us socially, sexually, vocationally, but to assess ourselves as we are now and to channel our energies and abilities effectively toward satisfactory accommodations to family, personal relationships, work, uses of leisure time.

Perhaps the place to begin is at the most basic level—how we function in the most intimate area of our lives, in our sexual behavior.

Chapter 5

ACTIVE VERSUS PASSIVE SEXUALITY

There is no reason why the milestone of the menopause should be expected to blunt the human female's sexual capacity, performance or drive. The healthy aging woman normally has sex drives that demand resolution. The depths of her sexual capacity and the effectiveness of her sexual performance, as well as her personal eroticism, are influenced indirectly by all of the psycho- and socio-physiologic problems of her aging process. In short, there is no time limit drawn by the advancing years to female sexuality.
—WILLIAM H. MASTERS and VIRGINIA E. JOHNSON,
Human Sexual Response

We were born in an era in which it was a disgrace for women to be sexually responsive. We matured in an era in which it was an obligation. We were caught between the "should nots" of a post-Victorian world and what Mary McCarthy called the "tyranny of the orgasm" of post-Freudian society. As in every other area of our lives, we are the women in the middle, firmly ensconced on the horns of the dilemmas and contradictions of our times.

We were taught *passivity* in sex. We were instructed on how to ignore our sexuality as children, avoid it as girls, acquiesce to it as young women, and now, suddenly, as mature women we are called upon both by the changing mores of our society and by the physiological realities of male and female sexuality in the middle years to modify or even abandon the responses, attitudes, the ways of thinking and acting sexually that we have lived with for all these years. Sex is suddenly no longer "something a man does to a woman"; if lovemaking is to be satisfactory for us, or perhaps even *possible* at this time of our lives, we may need to give ourselves sexual "permission" in a way that has been denied to us by our society and our own backgrounds in the past.

To see what we are up against, we might find it helpful first to consider what sexual permission is. Masters and Johnson define sexuality itself as "derived from sensory experiences individually invested with erotic meaning, which occur under the choice of circumstances and the influence of social values which make them convertible to and acceptable as sexual stimuli."

Sexual problems in women occur, the writers continue, when there is:

> . . . a stalemate in the socio-sexual adaptive process at the point in which a woman's desire for sexual expression crashes into a personal fear or conviction that her role as a sexual entity is without the unique contribution of herself as an individual. For some reason, her "permission" to function as a sexual being or her confidence as a functional sexual entity has been impaired.

To put it simply then, the way that we function has to do with how we translate what we are experiencing sexually according to the imprinting we have received early in our lives through subconscious conditioning (mainly through our parents) and then later by the psychosociology of our time and place. We are taught in our homes by society at large, sometimes directly and sometimes through subtle signals, how to *value* the sexual component of our personalities and how we can place it in the context of our lives. What was deemed right and proper in our homes when we were children and what has been called "ladylike" or "womanly" by our society determine the permission we give ourselves to enjoy sex and to integrate into our lives.

We have been given precious little permission by our society historically; that most of us have somehow managed to overcome the verbotens that were so relentlessly drilled into us is a triumph of our wills to grow, question, experience, experiment. Home, church, school enforced patterns of repression and denial of the sexual function. Rigid regulations are set determining the forms of acceptable sex: Masturbation is the sin of onanism; homosexuality is perversion; chastity is required before marriage and fidelity afterward.

Our literature romanticizes sexual repression and denial. Since the age of chivalry, there have been only two options for women: the whore and the madonna. "Good" women are nonsexual; their fallen sisters were punished with illegitimacy, ostracism, guilt. The puritan ethic denied *all* physical pleasure except possibly gluttony; sex was sinful.

We, the women in the middle, were given our initial sexual instruction by our mothers, whose sexual values were formed during the pre-World War I era, when women were assumed to be sexually neuter. This, of course, is not to say that all women until recently were frigid; what does seem to be true is that if in the privacy of her bedroom the post-Victorian woman *did* enjoy sex, she kept the information strictly to herself and imparted it, least of all, to her daughters. The word was: *Men* had "animal desires," although *gentlemen*—

past the age in which one sowed his wild oats with women of bad repute—kept them strictly under control. The marital bed was a place in which children were to be conceived; all else that occurred there was shrouded in shame and secrecy.

Inherent in this were two Biblical "permissions": Women were allowed to "serve men"—a wife's duty was to her husband—and they were also admonished to "bring forth children." Since women were created of a "finer clay" than men, part of their service involved the elevation of males to a level of purity closer to their own. Both servility and condescension were part of the female sex role. The message, brilliantly schizophrenic as it was, went something like this: Men were beasts, but one's conjugal duty required *acquiescence.* It also was women's place to *deny* men sex whenever possible. Women were permitted headaches, vapors and fatigue, frigidity, childbirth and female disorders, Lydia Pinkham's tonic, and the grateful end to sex with the onset of menopause. What they were not permitted was pleasure.

All this was supposedly changed with the advent of the First World War and the beginnings of psycho-analysis when, as psychiatrist Gregory Zilboorg writes:

> The mid-Victorian cast of chastity, innocent prudery, coyness and romantic passivity was dealt a . . . substantial blow. . . . True psychological equality with man, individual initiative, rank asser-tion of her right to choose a sexual partner instead of always being chosen and "kept" by a man—all this was truly revolutionary.

And yet, the more things change, as the French say, the more they remain the same. Dr. Zilboorg continues:

> Psychoanalysis, which almost from its inception dealt with the psychological difference between man and woman, has failed surprisingly to analyze this new shift in culture. . . . A perusal of the psychoanalytical literature between 1914 and the early twenties fails to disclose anything more than an occasional discussion of the biophysical differences between man and woman, which were accounted for by . . . the anatomical differences between the sexes. Psychoanalysis, which in all other aspects of human psychology was iconoclastic, seems to have resigned itself to this accepted decree of destiny.

What went wrong, of course, is that Freud postulated woman's sexuality as "inferior" on the grounds that women are biologically inferior to men since they do not possess penises. Freud's theories about women are so well known now through the literature of the current women's liberation movement that they barely need repeating; however, the brief summation in the Kinsey report puts them into useful focus: 1. *The nature of sexuality itself is masculine;* the "libido" or self-assertive drive is "phallic." 2. *Female organs are in themselves "incomplete";* female genitalia are actually "wounds" since the penis is absent. 3. *Female sexuality is passive* since the "mature" organ of sexual response is the vagina, a receptacle. (Freud recognized that "in the phallic phase of the girl, the clitoris is the dominant erotogenic zone. But . . . with the change to femininity, the clitoris must give up to

the vagina its sensitivity, and with it, its importance.")
4. *Aggressive-cliteroid-immature* (these traits are
lumped together, particularly in the work of such
disciples of Freud as Helene Deutsch) *women who
seek to deny men their masculinity*, are castrators.

Why Freud, the genius who gave the modern world
"permission" for sexuality, was so much a prisoner of
his Victorian world that he was forced to view women
through the pop culture of the day—passive, acquies-
cent, nonsexual—is less important than the fact that
his ideas prevailed and were trimmed and tailored by
later schools of psychoanalytic thought to fit the pop
culture of succeeding eras. Here is how the "anatomy
is destiny" theory of women's sexuality fits into the
"feminine mystique" years in which we were young
women, as explained in *Modern Woman: The Lost
Sex*, published in 1947.

The basic premise of the book is that the "biological" nature of women is "nutritive," women's function
being primarily childbearing and rearing. In modern
woman, this function has been undervalued; as she
"competes" with men for prestige, education, work
outside the home (all marks of penis envy, of course),
she loses her sexual capacity. Pleasure in sex for its
own sake is "masculine"; sexual freedom for women is
its own punishment:

> Failure to attain orgasm . . . is traceable either to
> the fact that woman has by stubborn, conscious
> direction forced herself into a sexual situation
> wherein she is not emotionally supported—or that
> she is unconsciously hostile to the act and rivalrous
> toward the male. . . . The woman needs to have in
> her unconscious mind the knowledge that for her

the sex act, to yield maximum satisfaction, termi-
nates only with childbirth. . . . Mere orgasm can
never be the entire sexual goal for a satisfactorily
functioning woman.

Now then, by the 1950's we had come full
circle—with an added set of instructions. We were, as.
in the past, permitted sexuality for procreation, we
were again told it was our duty to carry out the sex act,
but whereas previous generations were prohibited
from having orgasms (sexual responsiveness *wasn't
nice*), we were *obliged* to have them, in order to prove
that we were real *women*. Furthermore, we were
obliged to have them *vaginally* (look, Ma, no hands!)
to prove to ourselves that we were *mature* (the clitoris
being an immature organ) and to our men that they
were sexually potent. "Trying to make sure that the
man has an orgastic experience, and also wondering
whether she can have one herself," Bruno Bettelheim
writes in an essay called "Growing Up Female," "she
becomes so worried that she truly experiences little
satisfaction, and ends up pretending. Sexual intercourse cannot often bear the burden of proving so
many things in addition to being enjoyable." Hence,
the "tyranny of the orgasm."

But if the "modern sexuality" to which we had to
make our second adjustment was basically only a
variation of the traditional vision of women as less
sexual than men, there was soon to be a *real* change in
store for us: the psychosociology of the time in which
we live now. As mature women we have witnessed
three distinct periods of theory about female sexuality,
seen in most vivid relief in the roles assumed by
women in the theater: Compare Mary Pickford, the

innocent of the twenties, in her struggles to *preserve her chastity against the predatory male;* Doris Day, the heroine of the fifties, who deftly manipulated her virginity *to trap the amorous male;* and Janis Joplin, the funky, erotic, polysexual folk heroine of the sixties, who *owned her own sexuality, and used it frankly and openly for her own pleasure.*

What brought about the changeover is open to question; the first of the Kinsey books, *Sexual Behavior in the Human Female,* in its introduction, describes the twentieth century as:

> . . . a period of exceedingly rapid and revolutionary change in sex attitudes and practices. Whereas throughout the nineteenth century the puritanic attitude in sexual matters was dominant in the United States, since the turn of the century, both mores and practices have been in flux. What fifty years ago could not have been mentioned in a social group—sexual and reproductive happenings and experiences—are now spoken of without inhibition.

The report ascribes the changes to the influence of new psychoanalytic theories, to women's increasing economic and sexual emancipation, to the exposure of American youth during the world wars to cultures and peoples whose sex codes and practices differ from their own.

But perhaps the most significant factor was the publication of the book itself. The first large-scale scientific report on the nature of female sexuality, the survey used data collected from nearly 8,000 women and the combined expertise of specialists in every field of "medicine, biology, physiology, the social sciences, penology, marriage counseling, literature, the fine arts. . . ." Given the nature of the report, it was impossible for either specialists or the public at large to disregard its findings: the discovery that nearly all the assumptions about female sexuality to which we had previously ascribed were myths. The bombshell was this:

> In brief, we conclude that the anatomic structures which are most essential to sexual response and orgasm are nearly identical in the human female and male. The differences are relatively few. They are associated with the different functions of the sexes in reproductive processes, but they are of no great significance in the origins and development of sexual response and orgasm.

The Kinsey report debunked all the beliefs central to the role of passivity in women: the inadequacy of female genitalia; the idea that the range of female sexual practices—masturbation, sexual fantasies, behavior in homosexual and heterosexual activity—was narrower than that of males. The results of the report contradicted the notion that it was the "feminine" woman who was truly a "woman" sexually; the report confirmed the findings of psychologist Dr. Abraham Maslow, who had written a decade earlier:

> [It is] our high dominance women [who] feel more akin to men than to women in tastes, attitudes, prejudices, aptitudes, philosophy and inner personality . . . the self actualized woman who has the full use and exploitation of talents, capacities, potentialities . . . who [finds] sex can be wholeheartedly enjoyed. . . .

The scientists stated flatly that the normal woman is far from being disadvantaged sexually; indeed, she has the capacity for multiple orgasms and prolonged sexual enjoyment. The "differences" between the "clitoral" and the "vaginal" orgasm are nonexistent; there is one orgasm, regardless of the physiological stimulation, a conclusion that meant women need no longer require themselves to find satisfaction in ways almost guaranteed not to permit it, in order to fill male expectations. But more profound was the underlying theme of Masters' and Johnson's therapeutic approach to sexual problems: *Men and women find fullest sexual pleasure in sexual behavior that is not role-defined* —that is to say, it occurs when each partner assumes both active and passive participation. The "feminine" woman who remains the recipient, who does not give herself permission to initiate sexual activity, to know about her own body and to explore her lover's—in a word, to function as a full partner—is, in fact, the sexually deprived woman.

Reviewing the diverse amalgam that is the psychosocial background of our own sexuality, I wondered how we as mature women fit in. While we do not make a conscious effort to conform to changing standards, the climate does alter our behavior. We are told that seduction is desirable—a "smart" wife retains the "aura of allure," so we buy black lace nightgowns, put lipstick on before breakfast. We hear that "women's lib" is "threatening" to men; we worry about the "growing plague" of male impotence; we worry about being "too sexual." My questions were: Against the background of our individual sexual learning, how have we handled our sexual relationships until now, how do we feel about ourselves as sexual beings, and how do our attitudes and experiences serve us now, in our middle years?

To find what I wanted to know, I drew from my own experiences and from what I learned during many hours of talking with some sixty women who volunteered to answer my questions. I found, first, a significant change in attitudes as a result of the sexual revolution of this decade; women now talk easily and openly about sex. I could not help contrasting the apparent frankness of the women's conversations with the guarded talk I had heard at bull sessions in the college dormitory twenty-five years earlier ("Do you think *she* goes all the way?" we would whisper conspiratorially, while staunchly defending our *own* virginity) and with conversations I had had as a young woman with other young matrons in my circle in which "good taste" demanded that one didn't talk too much about "what goes on in the privacy of the bedroom." I found, this time, women were willing and even anxious to discuss their fears and problems, their satisfactions and pleasures.

Beginning the interviews, I found that women's memories of their earliest sexual feelings and imprintings supported the belief that sex is "dirty" and that the possession of sexual apparatus was shameful. There was one event that took place in the lives of every single woman with whom I spoke: an incident, either masturbatory, self-investigative, or in sex play with other children in which she had been made to understand that what she was doing was "naughty." Sexual curiosity was off bounds, and the message was impressed in subtle ways—" 'That's not nice,' my mother told me," or " 'Only bad girls do that' "—and sometimes in traumatic ways: "I was caught playing doctor and got a spanking." Almost equally shared was the feeling of embarrassment about their anatomy: "I remember being told that I was old enough to bathe myself, and being told to be sure to wash 'down there,' and I felt funny about touching myself with the cloth." There were variations on this theme: "I didn't think much about my body sexually. It seemed pretty neuter to me until my breasts began to develop. Breasts marked me as female—everything else was sort of a blank." A number of women recalled that their early interest in their anatomy had been squelched by parental disapproval, and although some women spoke of having secretly examined themselves or their friends, the majority seemed to have no clear memories of when they learned anatomical facts about them-selves; in fact, I sensed that some of the women *still* found their own anatomy fairly mysterious.

Going into attitudes in girlhood and young adult-hood, I began to encounter much more diversity. What seemed fairly common, though, was the hard struggle with external pressures about sexuality rather than internal ones. Boys seemed much more sexual; there was the problem of keeping boys at bay, of rationing out sexual behavior: "I knew it was the girl who had to set the limits." There was the awareness of avoiding danger: "I was afraid of being 'forced'; I didn't want to tease, but it was so easy to get boys excited." Fear of pregnancy was mentioned frequently: "I didn't want to 'get caught'" (the euphemism for pregnancy), but more than that, there were the social pressures for chastity to which Masters and Johnson refer:

> During her formative years the female dissembles much of her developing functional sexuality in

response to social requirements for a "good girl" façade. Instead of being taught or allowed to value her sexual feelings in anticipation of appropriate and meaningful opportunity for expression, thereby developing a realistic sexual value system, she must attempt to repress or remove them from their natural context of environmental stimulation. . . . She is allowed to retain the symbolic romanticism which usually accompanies these sexual feelings, but the concomitant sensory development with the symbolism that endows the sexual value system with meaning is arrested or labeled—for the wrong reasons—objectionable.

I saw constant evidence of the "symbolic romanticism." Since what I wanted to know was the way women felt about themselves sexually and how they integrated their sexuality in their lives, rather than data on actual experience, number and variety of "outlets," incidence of orgasms, and other material that I could not either measure or evaluate, I asked for no statistics about premarital intercourse. I did, however, get the impression that most of the women with whom I spoke had either no premarital experience or very little. It was "falling in love" that preoccupied them, rather than sex itself. "I wanted to save myself for the man I love" seemed to be a common theme.

I asked women about their feelings during the early years of marriage against the background of Kinsey's research: Among women in our generation, nearly half experienced orgasms within the first month of marriage, and that figure rose steadily so that more than three-fourths were orgastic by the end of their first year. The figures proved almost irrelevant, however; most women seemed to evaluate their sexual happiness not so much in terms of physical response as they did in compatibility. It was love and closeness that they stressed—sexual love, not orgasms.

Nevertheless, my major findings again tied in with Kinsey's research: The sex drive of the male in the twenties and thirties is higher than the female's. By and large women told me that during the early years of marriage their husbands desired sex more frequently than they did; there was a real pattern of "slow awakening." A number of women spoke about not feeling "wooed." "It was always slam-bam, thank you, ma'am," one said caustically. "We made love in the dark, and I thought he felt the quicker it was over, the better." Other women spoke about the fact that they made love on demand: "I always thought I shouldn't say no, not even when I wasn't in the mood."

Individual differences emerged strongly; there were women who said that their sex urges were easily as strong as those of their husbands. "It was always easy to excite him," said one who gave me a fairly graphic description of her seductive technique. "I always knew sex was available to me when I wanted it, and I still do." But in the main, I heard that the years in which women were occupied with childbearing and rearing were those in which their interest in sexual activity was low. Physical fatigue, children's demands were mentioned often: "Every time we began to make love one of the kids woke up crying." Or, "I was so exhausted that by the time I got in bed all I wanted to do was sleep."

Because the "permission" women receive for sexuality is so tied in with procreation, I wanted to know what the act of conception itself meant to the women in terms of sexual emotion. A few women told me that their desire to have children was an outgrowth of sexual joy and love: "Making love was so beautiful, I knew I wanted to complete it by having a child." But by and large, I felt that the idea that a woman reaches her highest sexuality in the desire for a child and the act of conception was an illusion. Even when conception was planned, rather than accidental, it did not seem to carry any additional sexual pleasure for most women. And for many, the fear of unwanted pregnancy or conversely, the difficulty for the less fertile in conceiving added burdens to the problem of achieving sexual happiness.

Before bringing up to the present time into the middle years what I had learned from research and heard from women, I again went back to Kinsey and Masters and Johnson. Here is Kinsey's summation of the sexual responsiveness of women of our generation through the years: During the first years of marriage, nearly 100 percent of women were having marital coitus. After age thirty, the percentage begins to drop; between age thirty-one and thirty-five it is 98 percent, but after age fifty-five, only 80 percent. In terms of the frequency of marital relations, the figures are more sharply defined. As newlyweds, on an average the women of our generation had coitus nearly 3 times a week; by age thirty, 2.2 times per week; at age forty, 1.5 times per week; at age fifty, once a week; and at age 60, only once every twelve days. And finally, surveying incidence of orgasm: The highest incidence is between ages thirty-one and forty, when 90 percent of women are responding. From age forty-one, the number of women who experience orgasm begins to drop: Only 78 respond orgastically in their early fifties, and then only 65 percent by their late fifties.

The picture seems clear; after age thirty, we not only make love less often, but apparently—using orgasm as measure—enjoy it less too.

And yet the picture that I got from talking to women did not support the idea of a lowered sexuality in the middle years. It was just the contrary! With only two exceptions, every woman I interviewed who was between the ages of forty and fifty described herself as less inhibited, more willing to enjoy sex, and more physically responsive than she had been at any other time in her life! It was only after age fifty that I saw a diminishing of this pattern, and even at that, many women well into their late fifties still spoke about a high plateau of sexual feeling.

What was it that they said? First, most of the women with whom I spoke ascribed their increased interest in sex to one or more of these changes: more time and leisure; more privacy with the children grown and on their own; a changing zeitgeist, the feeling of the times that has at last made sexuality "respectable" or at least not shameful; some intrinsic change within themselves, which they described as "increased confidence" in themselves, a general "letting go," a willingness to take pleasure for themselves that they had previously denied. Here in the words of a forty-year-old writer, the wife of a psychologist, who was my most articulate interviewee, are some of the feelings that other women hinted at: "You discover your sexuality as you go along, the way that you begin to discover all the facets of your being—through experience. It's not just a discovery that you make about yourself in bed; it's everywhere, the sense of power you gain through understanding other people, through observing how men—not only your husband, but all the men that you come in contact with socially and professionally—respond to you. As I've grown, become more of a person, my sexuality, which is part of my totality, has grown too."

Some women spoke about their increased sexuality as a result of many years of sexual relations with their husbands. They had finally achieved a comfortable familiarity: "I used to have to have a drink, or take a warm bath to relax before I made love. Sometimes I enjoyed sex, and other times I just went along with it for my husband's sake. But now I really look forward to it. I respond all the time, with no strain." Although the problem of boredom with marital sex relations— the tedium of the same partner—seems to be part of men's jokes about themselves and is written about by both Kinsey and Masters and Johnson, I heard very few women complain that sex had become humdrum through lack of variety. Familiarity had a positive effect on most women's sexuality: "We know how to please each other now. I think sex gets better as time goes on."

A number of women mentioned lack of fear of pregnancy as having made the difference in their feelings. Menopause and better birth control methods were mentioned: "I feel safe now." A few spoke of "hormonal" change: "I think something just happens to a body at a certain age." Quite a few women told me, one way or another, that they thought it was sex, not youth, that's wasted on the young: "When I think of all the years that I wasted, I could kick myself. I'm ready for love all the time now."

At what age, I wondered, do women feel a real decline in their sexual capacities? It was hard for me to tell, because I was unable to separate lack of opportunity from lack of desire; among the older women there were increased numbers who were not living with husbands and who were not involved intimately with men. The answers that I did get were diverse: One woman approaching sixty, who had been very forthright during our long interview, told me, "When you're married thirty-five years, you don't find sex very important." Although her marriage was very satisfactory, she thought of her husband as a companion rather than a lover; their sexual relationship was nearly nonexistent. But another woman, a fifty-seven-year-old grandmother, told me that her marriage was still strongly sexual—and she knocked on wood when she told me her husband was "still all there."

The last response struck a familiar chord. It confirmed the findings of Masters and Johnson, who, in *Human Sexual Inadequacy,* present the only authentic study that we have of the sexual functioning of mature women. This is what they have to say:

> The misconceptions, fallacies, and even taboos directed toward the sexual functioning of women in menopausal and post menopausal years are legion. Knowledge of natural variations in the female sexual cycle developing with the aging process has been extremely limited. . . .We must, in fact, destroy the concept that women in the 50–70 year age group not only have no interest in but also have no facility for active sexual expression. Nothing could be further from the truth than the often-expressed concept that aging women do not maintain a high level of sexual orientation.

In their studies, Masters and Johnson distinguish between women who continue to have active sex lives well into later years and those who don't.

> There are many variations . . . but two distinct patterns are seen most frequently. The first response pattern is the well-established one of women who terminate menstrual flow in their late forties or early fifties, yet continue with reduced clinically apparent sex-steroid production for years thereafter. These women have few if any menopausal symptoms. . . . Their high levels of strength and energy, in contrast to that of their peers, is obvious to the most casual observer. . . . Effective sexual functioning continues unabated . . . and their [organs] retain a significant degree of configuration of the younger woman.
>
> The second pattern has been established by older women regularly having intercourse once or twice a week and having done so over a period of many years. There is tremendous physiological, and of course psychological value in continuity of sexual exposure. . . . To a significant degree, regularity of sexual exposure will overcome the influence of sex-steroid inadequacy in the female pelvis. . . .

In contrast, Masters and Johnson describe women who have not had regular sexual relations during the years as showing evidence of physical atrophy and loss of zest and energy.

The evidence seems clear on the basis of laboratory research: Women's capacity for sexual participation and enjoyment does not diminish with the years. In fact, sexual activity provides an added bonus of good physical and mental health for women in the middle years. Certainly from my interviews, I could hardly fail to agree; even making allowances for what I was hearing in terms of the fact that there is a natural tendency for an interviewer to find the answer she has anticipated, I could not help assessing women's sexuality in the middle years as strong and vigorous. Why, then, do the Kinsey figures show diminished sexual activity for women at the very time that their needs are for increased participation?

The answer came from the Kinsey report itself, from the interviews that I had with women, and from an assessment of our psychosociological background. Kinsey's explanation is most cogent. Studying the broad spectrum of women's sexual range—for example, masturbation, homosexual activity, extramarital coitus, as well as sexual activity within marriage—Kinsey found *that it is only marital coitus that shows a "steady decline with advancing age."* Comparisons of male and female statistics, as well as comparisons of female sexual activity *other* than marital coitus, indicate "no evidence that the female ages in her sexual capacities." The report concludes that "the steady decline in the incidences and frequencies of marital coitus from the younger to the older age groups must be the product of the aging process in the male." In other words, *contrary to our own sexual needs, which "rise to their maximum point [during the middle years] and stay more or less on level until after 55 or 60 years of age," we are forced into marital sex patterns that are in line with the biological and social needs of men, not women.*

What seems a cruel trick of nature—the fact that sex is most available to us when we want and need it least, and least available at the time that our needs are strongest—is further explained by Kinsey:

> One of the tragedies which appears in a number of marriages originates in the fact that the male may be most desirous of sexual contact in his early years, while the responses of the female are still undeveloped, and while she is still struggling to free herself from the acquired inhibitions which prevent her from participating freely in the marital activity. But over the years most females become less inhibited and develop an interest in sexual relations which they may then maintain until they are in their fifties and even sixties. But by then the responses of the average male may have dropped so considerably that his interest in coitus, especially . . . with a wife who has previously objected to the frequencies of his requests, may have sharply declined.

What seems clear, then, is that now, in our middle years, we reap the harvest of a lifetime of conflicts around our sexuality, of acceptance of the passive role in which we were to be pursued, made love to, if not actually against our will, at very least without our active enthusiasm. As this harvest falls due in synchronization with our men's physiological decline sexually (unlike the sexual experiences of women, those of men in all areas, including masturbation, homosexual and extramarital experience, show a steady decline after the middle twenties, with a sharp falling off in the middle years), we are faced with the difficulty of reconciling our own needs and wishes with what is actually possible for us to achieve.

Although the women expressed it in different ways, much of what I heard reflected this problem. I listened to a number of women who felt personally rejected, did not understand that lowered sexuality is a part of the normal male pattern. "I don't excite him the way I used to," one woman explained in a heartbroken voice. Accustomed to viewing her desirability in terms of youth and beauty, she was convinced that her "aging" was cooling her husband's ardor. Many women spoke about feeling insecure about their appearance, and even those who had ample evidence that they were, in fact, sexually desirable, seemed troubled by inner doubts. In some corner of their minds they had never surmounted the early training that taught them that their bodies were unattractive, and now that the beauty of youth had faded, they felt they were increasingly unattractive. Other women hinted that they thought their husbands were having extramarital affairs, and that was the factor that accounted for less interest in them; the fear of infidelity on the part of husbands seems to be among the most pervasive and tormenting fears of the middle years. Some women seemed stubbornly committed to the wooing patterns of earlier years: "If I'm not pursued, I don't feel sexy." Or, "I only feel like a woman when I'm being, well—*taken.*"

Despite the fears of the foes of women's liberation, the problem didn't seem to me to be that women are "too aggressive"; what I heard women say was that the lifetime patterns they had developed—submissiveness and passivity—were serving them poorly at this time in their lives when their partners' diminishing sexuality required increased seductiveness and even aggressiveness. It seemed to me that many women with whom I spoke were experiencing some degree of frustration in their sexual relationships, were dimly aware of the fact that there was "something" they could do, but either didn't quite know how to do it or were afraid of losing their femininity.

Given all the obstacles to pleasurable and satisfying sexuality—antisexual conditioning and a sexual timetable in which the needs and compatibilities of men and women are out of synchronization through what appear to be biological factors—what are the possibilities for accommodation in this area? Among the women with whom I spoke there were those who had achieved workable solutions, and although they varied in method, what they seemed to have in common was simply *flexibility*—the ability to break out of accustomed role patterns and habits and to develop new ways of coping.

I encountered women who spoke of a wide range of sexual attitudes and practices. Some were highly avant-garde—solutions that most women would be unlikely even to listen to comfortably, let alone to experiment with. Two women with whom I spoke were involved in "open marriages"; they did not see sexual fidelity as necessary to marital happiness, but rather as an actual block to it. "We were faithful to each other for thirty years," one woman explained, "or at least I was—he had some small affairs and felt guilty and secretive about them. We feel secure enough to experiment now. We've each had affairs in the past couple of years, we've been truthful with each other about that, and they've given our marriage zest and variety—and sexual stimulation." The second woman had gone through a period of mutually accepted nonfidelity and now thought she had satisfied her curiosity and was returning to fidelity.

But most of the women who had achieved comfortable sexuality in the middle years spoke about more conventional solutions. "I don't wait to be swept off my feet anymore; that belongs to the past. What we have now is a sort of mutual understanding. When I feel in the mood, I make overtures, and if our lovemaking is cuddling and closeness instead of sex, that's OK." Other women spoke about introducing variety and experimentation into their marriage. "I'm glad that we're in a franker age now. You'd be surprised how many ideas I get from the movies and books I read!" None of the women spoke about "tricks"—the methods of *The Sensual Woman* were only amusing to them—but the underlying theme that I heard connected with sexual success at this time seemed to run something like this: "I've reached the age where I see myself as having to take responsibility for sex in a way that I didn't years ago. If sex is to be pleasurable, I know I have to be willing and able to do my part."

It was this willingness to take the responsibility for full partnership that seemed to me to be part of the sexual pattern of women who spoke of finding satisfaction in their present sex lives. They told me they thought that the familiarity they now had with their own bodies and psyches, the long-term association with their partners made for an ease not possible earlier in their lives. But more than that, in growing toward active sexuality, in discarding the passive, self-renunciative role that has been the behavior appropriate to women, they had learned to make sex a cooperative activity and to find new depths of meaning in closeness, warmth, and affection. They had overcome the formidable obstacles to self-realization that is the handicap not only to sexual fulfillment, but to marriage as well.

Chapter 6

THE SEPARATE WORLDS OF MARRIAGE

The ache of marriage . . .

We look for communion
and are turned away, beloved,
each and each. . .
looking for joy, some joy
not to be known outside it

two by two in the ark of
the ache of it.
—DENISE LEVERTOV, The Ache of Marriage

There is hardly any way to escape it. We are assailed on all sides by the most fashionable topic of the year—the future of the family. On talk shows and in the movies, at parties and symposiums, the subject seems to preempt almost everything else: Will marriage survive the inroads into our social, political, ecological, and sexual order that the seventies are bringing? And yet, in the face of the debate, we women in our middle years are a generation wholly committed to traditional marriage. More than 90 percent of us have been married at some time in our lives, and despite the spiraling divorce rates in the decade between forty and fifty, eight out of ten of us live with husbands, while even at age sixty-four more than six out of ten are still married.

As a group we are only peripherally interested in questions about whether the institution will survive, change form, or vanish; what interests us is how we can, at this time in our lives, continue to deal constructively with the conflicts and problems within the traditional marriage format to which the vast majority of us are committed.

It is a cliche to say that marriage in the middle years is the summation of all that has come before. We have faced formidable odds against happiness and fulfillment from the very beginning of our marriages, for beyond such obvious pitfalls as conflicts over money, sex, in-laws, child rearing, there are the most profound obstacles to successful marriage. We were taught even as children that we were not to merge; we were to "complement" each other. Males and females have instilled in them ways of recognizing and expressing emotion differently, are programmed to assume role patterns vocationally and in marriage that barely overlap, and as part of the proof of our "masculinity" and "femininity" required to erect barriers to the most important factors necessary to union: intimacy and compromise.

Looking backward, we find that the problems began for us about the time we were presented with our Keepsake Diamonds. The men and women of our generation embarked on lifetime partnerships in which each principal had a separate vision of the reasons for entering into the union, a totally divergent set of needs to be satisfied by the merger, and a wholly different view of what the business itself was to be. Moreover, neither partner had the faintest idea of what the other's expectations or assumptions were, and as part of the contract neither discussed the matter prior to the arrangement, nor was there to be much airing of it afterward. We went into "his" marriage and "her" marriage, with the mistaken illusion that it was to be "our" marriage.

The Kinsey report, not ordinarily given to social commentary, nevertheless names the game in this case. "Most men marry for sexual reasons," the book says baldly, "while women marry for love, security and a home." With that finding accepted as an axiom of marriage, it doesn't take much imagination to anticipate the basic difficulties that will ensue. As Julius Fast explains, the male vision, or what he calls the "James Bond fantasy, simply does not include Mrs. Goodhousekeeping as the bedmate of 007. So, while Joe projects himself into the American masculine daydream, Ann wanders, lost, on the road between Betty Crocker's kitchen and the pad of the sensuous woman." Hence, as Fast concludes, they are involved in an arrangement predicated on the "basic incompatibility of men and women."

The paths to both the James Bond fantasy and the gingham world of Mrs. Goodhousekeeping begin well before the Christmas when Santa brings Sonny a gun and Sister a plug-in iron. Boys and girls are literally brought up with the expectation that they will be incompatible. As part of acceptable "masculine" behavior, boys are denied the ability even to verbalize feelings, much less actually to allow themselves the sensitivity to another's feelings—particularly those of the *"opposite"* sex—that would enable them to share in the most intimate of all human relationships. The male image requires boys to be strong and silent, unconcerned with the petty details of interpersonal relationships. Young males are instructed in ways of barricading their feelings even from themselves; emotion itself is off bounds.

If tenderness, communication, interest and sympathy for people are beyond the pale of acceptable male behavior, other behavior traits necessary for honest expression and interaction are denied to women. From childhood, girls are taught to conceal anger and aggression, to be manipulative. "Stand up and fight it out," we tell our sons; our daughters are tutored to believe that honey catches more flies than vinegar. The end result is that boys grow up suspicious of girls' deviousness; women fear men's brutality.

Superimposed upon these acceptable modes of feeling and expression for males and females are corresponding patterns of both social and sexual behavior. Males are encouraged to wander, to test themselves abroad; girls are trained to stay close to home, to care for and protect themselves—and eventually, others—to seek acceptance and satisfaction from those closest to them. The home itself is a trap for males, a nest and shelter for females. The Thurber cartoon in *The Battle of the Sexes* shows a terrified man running away from a house whose outline suggests the form of a crouching woman threatening to engulf him. And why not? "G'wan home, your mother's calling" rings as a taunt in the ears of males until at last it is exorcised: "Got áway from the old ball and chain tonight."

Nor do sexual mores permit the possibility of easy, comfortable mutuality. Boys are taught to woo in order to collect the prize—sex; girls are instructed on how to offer the bait—sex—in order to be wooed. "Gee," my high school swain complained, "after I bought you hot dogs and paid for all the rides!" "I always make sure that he courts me first," my friend's mother-in-law told her, describing a pattern of lovemaking—or perhaps sexual blackmail—that had obtained during the forty years of her marriage.

But in spite of the years of prenuptial power play and what would seem to be total familiarity with the rules of the game, neither partner seems to be able to see through the sham. It doesn't occur to girls who have been instructed from puberty that "boys are only after one thing" that the motivating factor for men entering marriage is a steady, assured source of sexual satisfaction. Even the thought is degrading. Nor, evidently, do men who have observed women guard themselves against sexuality really come to grips with the idea that this behavior and training are likely to engender a distrust for the sexual side of marriage. Every prospective bride harbors in her mind the belief that *deep down* her fiance is as interested as she in feathering a nest, ordering wedding invitations, selecting silver patterns, and eventually buying a home in the suburbs, while every man is happily anticipating the wedding night when his bride will confess that all she really wants is a couch of twigs in the woods for orgies *a deux* with him. The only sensible way to mask these diversities is behind the kindly veil of romantic love. "He loves me for myself," girls assure themselves, never asking what that means; love, after all, conquers all.

Underlying much of the incompatibility between men and women is our society's acceptance of the double standard, "a code of morals," as the *Oxford Dictionary* forthrightly defines it, "that imposes a strict standard of behavior on women but allows men greater freedom." In sexual morality, the double standard begins with the permission given to the adolescent male to sow his wild oats and the restriction placed on the female to remain chaste. Men are "biologically" the roving impregnators, women the faithful nest builders. Then, oddly, with marriage, a new kind of biological imperative is expected to emerge. Every bride of my generation entered marriage with the absolute conviction that her husband would be faithful; every groom believed that his wife would prove to be so gratifying a sexual partner that he would never stray.

The oddity about the double standard is that it is strangely at variance with American moral codes—we are historically an equalitarian society based on the puritan work ethic which is opposed to hedonism; it is in the Latin countries that men have traditionally been allowed to lunch with their mistresses and dine with their wives. And yet it applies as consistently to sexual morality in Grand Rapids as it does in Paris or Palermo—the difference being that we have evolved a kind of surreptitious schizophrenia about it. Men and women fail to acknowledge the possibility beforehand that one of those "nights out with the boys" will actually become a night out with a girl, and when it actually does occur, it will be kept hidden not only from the wife, but in some corner of the husband's mind, from himself. The Kinsey report itself confesses to some bafflement on this issue:

> Society knows that extra-marital intercourse does occur, and that it occurs with some frequency, and it seems not to matter that it is generally known that such intercourse usually goes unpunished. Society is still outraged when confronted with the specific case on which it is challenged to pass judgment. . . . These social attitudes are particularly interesting in view of the fact that a considerable proportion of those who react most violently against

the known instances of extra-marital relations may
have similar experience in their own histories. . . .
Considering that the legal penalties for such sexual
activity are rarely enforced, and that most males feel
that such activity is highly desirable and not exactly
wrong, it is particularly interesting to observe this
considerable disturbance over the issue.

The secret rules of the fidelity game, then, go
something like this: Fidelity, in spite of the fact that it
actually seems to occur less often than not, is
considered an absolute necessity in a marriage;
moreover, it is the single most important criterion on
which the success or failure of a marriage is judged.
"Was he unfaithful?" we ask when we hear of an
impending divorce, as though fidelity were the
bedrock of marriage. To wives, fidelity continues to
hold this status; confronted with the possibility of a
husband's infidelity, a woman sees three choices:
Either she can decide "what I don't know won't hurt
me" and discard the evidence, or she can accept it and
live with a "ruined" marriage. The last choice, of
course, is divorce.

For men, the game goes this way: One loves one's
wife, but it is "in a man's nature" to be unfaithful. The
infidelity "means nothing" but neverthcless must be
kept from the wife, for "it would hurt her" (women do
not understand men's emotions and needs). The
infidelity is at once a source of pleasure and guilt; one
is proud of oneself for being a swinger and bitterly
ashamed for being a liar and a cheat. The fact that it is
hidden and covered with lies and evasions is both
exciting and uncomfortable. Forbidden fruit is sweet-
est, but the wife who requires the lie is a nuisance.

For women, infidelity is an entirely different matter. In the first place, both the social and legal penalties are extreme; historically, infidelity is excusable in a man, but he may "put his wife away" for her indiscretions. There is no female equivalent of a "casual affair"; we are brought up with the belief that while men can copulate casually, women require love as a condition of sexual fulfillment. There is surely no social approval from one's peers; a man who "gets away with it" is the object of secret admiration from "the boys." Learning of a sister's extramarital affairs, "the girls" are more likely to feel pity than envy; what disappointment in the marriage, they wonder, has driven her to such an accommodation?

Reviewing the startlingly different expectations, attitudes, and emotional needs that are fostered by society upon men and upon women, the divergent standards of behavior, the diametrically opposed roles the sexes are taught to assume, the wonder grows that there is any belief in the wish that these denizens of different worlds can ever pair off. The way in which this works out is through a series of metaphors in which the marital arrangements are camouflaged by the partners themselves.

Betty Friedan has pointed out the prevailing metaphor for marriage among the women of our generation. Self-development, self-exploration, the building of independence were given negative social value for women; one was to achieve adult womanhood by "giving" and "loving" others—a husband, children. Philip Roth, in an excerpt from his novel *My Life as a Man*, presents the corresponding male metaphor for marriage in these remarks by the book's protagonist, Peter Tarnopol.

. . . For those young men who reached their maturity in the fifties . . . there was considerable moral prestige in taking a wife, and hardly because a wife was going to be one's maidservant or sexual "object." Decency and Maturity, a young man's "seriousness" were at issue precisely because it was thought to be the other way around: in that the great world was so obviously a man's, it was only *within* marriage that a woman could hope to find equality and dignity. Indeed, we were led to believe . . . that we were exploiting and degrading the women we *didn't* marry rather than those we did.' . . . It was up to us then to give them the value and purpose that society at large withheld—by marrying them.

No wonder then that a young college-educated bourgeois male of my generation who scoffed at the idea of marriage for himself, who would just as soon eat out of cans or in cafeterias, sweep his own floor, make his own bed, and come and go with no binding legal attachments, finding female friendship and sexual adventure where and when he could, and for no longer than he liked, lay himself open to the charge of "immaturity" if not "latent" or blatant "homosexuality." Or he could not "commit himself" (nice enough institutional phrase, that) to "a permanent relationship." Worst of all, most shameful of all, the chances were that this person who thought he was perfectly able to take care of himself on his own was in actuality "unable to love."

An awful lot of worrying was done in the fifties about whether people were able To Love or not—I venture to say, much of it by young women in behalf of the young men who didn't particularly want them to wash their socks and cook their meals and bear their children, and tend them for the rest of their natural days. "But aren't you capable of Loving anyone? Can't you think of anyone but yourself?"

when translated from desperate fifties-feminese into plain English, generally meant, "I want to get married and I want you to get married to."

According to Roth's Peter Tarnopol, the separate worlds of men and women are not even served by the same language; the woman's metaphor is spoken in "feminese." Nor are these worlds likely to be bridged *after* marriage, for the institution itself brings completely different rewards and disappointments to each sex. For the women of my generation, marriage was the culmination of girlhood dreams, conferring upon us security, status, friends. It was an escape from the restrictions of childhood: sexual, social, economic. It was "a home of one's own"—autonomy as well as shelter.

Marriage brought us society's approval; it was an achievement to have "caught a man," to secure him so that the world knew we'd made it. It was the way in which we discharged our duty to our own parents and officially entered the estate not only of womanhood, but of equality with our own mothers. "You made the kitchen curtains yourself!" my grandmother marveled at my first apartment; her subsequent gifts, hemstitched tea towels and a set of mixing bowls, were the chalice that passed between us.

For our husbands, however, the first years of marriage did not spell the attainment of youthful fantasies, but rather their forfeiture. Gone was the sense of freedom and autonomy for which they had fought with their parents since adolescence; as they once had to inform their mothers of their wereabouts, they were now accountable to their wives. Nor is there tribal approval from other males. "Wedding bells are breaking up that old gang of mine," the boys mourn.

No one admires *his* engagement ring; his pride in his wife-to-be is diluted with a certain shamefaced admission that yes, he *did* get hooked after all. And it is career achievement, not marriage, that will give him adulthood and status, that will admit him to par with his father. A boy's parents may be relieved to see him "settle down," but his father will offer him respect and status for making money, not love.

The separate worlds in which husbands and wives live is documented cogently by authors Roderick Thorp and Robert Blake, whose survey of what "American husbands really think of themselves, their wives, marriages, children, jobs, sex, divorce, and life in general" was published in the *Ladies' Home Journal*, July, 1973. "In the course of these interviews," the authors reported:

> We discovered two important differences in interviewing husbands as compared to wives. . . . First, the men had more mobility, but no genuine privacy. The interviews could not be done at home (because the wife was there) or at the office (because it was not private enough). As a result many of our in-depth conversations had to be conducted in automobiles, on lunch hours, or during free hours on business trips.
>
> The second difference was the fear that some men showed . . . many agreed to be interviewed, then failed to keep the appointments. None of the women . . . did that. Of course, as we discovered when we finally sat down and talked to these reluctant men, some of them had good reason to be afraid.

The authors leave it, somewhat cryptically, at that. Reading the interviews for the first time, I jumped to the obvious conclusion: The "good reason" for fear was infidelity. In the ten interviews published, four men spoke outright of affairs; these included one in which there was one episode, set up to "spite" the wife, and one interview in which constant infidelity was justified on the grounds that "it's in the blood. . . . I don't know if I could stop playing around if I wanted to. . . ."

But going back over the interviews several times, I began to find far more complex and subtle reasons for men's fear. What they seemed to be expressing, sometimes angrily, sometimes begrudgingly, sometimes shamefacedly, and in one case quite openly, was a fear of the *dependency* of marriage, of the *intimacy*, of their *vulnerability*. The machismo pattern underlay everything they said; a man is expected to *make it work*. There is a pervasive sense of humiliation in the knowledge that it is a *woman* who can supply them with the approbation, the affirmation of their masculinity that they need, and that in order to receive it, they have to play what they consider a woman's game. Their relationships with other men are superficial, competitive. "It's not possible for a man like me to develop strong friendships with my colleague," one man explained typically. Nor did any of them indicate close emotional ties with their children; fatherhood itself was satisfying, as a part of the adult male role, but it was their wives to whom alternately, with need and resentment, that they needed to turn for personhood.

In a description by one of the men of his parents' marriage, I sensed his irritation and perhaps feeling of bafflement about his own;

Well, but my father's dead now, but he had a full, happy life. After the First World War he came over from Scotland with several thousand dollars and put it all into real estate. . . . He . . . put up a couple of houses and sold them, bought more land, built more houses, and just kept going from there. . . . When the depression came, he was ready. He made more money in the thirties than he did in the twenties, and still more in the forties. For as long as I could remember, he had people vying for his attention— and many were beautiful women. . . . Did my mother know? Oh, I think she did, but since the money was coming in all the time, she probably didn't want to rock the boat. She wasn't bitter. My father gave me everything she wanted.

Why, then, he seems to be asking, is his own life so complicated; why can't a woman be content with what she seems to have bargained for, a home, family, security, and money, and leave him free to the "real" world of success and adventure, while at the same time supplying him with the home base he needs? Several of the men spoke guardedly in this vein; it was unfair for their wives to make demands, particularly *emotional demands* they found difficult or embarrassing to meet. Many of them preferred to think of their wives as materialistic: "If I left her, she'd wipe me out." It was easier to think that marriage was a cool, hard bargain in which money counted, rather than as a profoundly intimate merging for which they were emotionally unequipped.

Reversing the coin, from interviews with women about their concepts of marriage, it seems that intimacy, closeness is what women desire, not the part of marriage from which they flee. "She's a good wife, I suppose, a good housekeeper and a good mother, but. . ." has no feminine equivalent; I've never heard a woman begin by saying, "He's a good husband, he's good to the children, and he's a good provider, but. . ." The security and financial support that a husband provides are taken for granted in a sense; it is the emotional sustainment which is the barometer of a marriage. Mary McCarthy, in *Memories of a Catholic Girlhood*, speaks of her grandmother's "archaic" view of the function of a husband: " 'But why did you pick Grandpa instead of one of the others?' " I pressed her. . . . 'Oh, I don't know, Mary,' she said, yawning. . . . She thought he would be good to her, she finally conceded." Men continue to think in ways, then, that are "archaic" to women or that, more directly, don't make sense.

The "incompatibility" of men and women is seen most clearly in our folk humor. "Do you love me?" she queries endlessly. "Of course I love you. I married you, didn't I?" The nagging question really asks, "Am I anything more than 'good to you'? Am I more than the person who keeps your home, rears your children, satisfies your sexual needs? Am I a person unique, precious in my own right?" The brisk answer says, "Don't torment me with questions that are painful and embarrassing to me, that require that I say I am not the powerful male, captain of industry, freewheeling adventurer, master of my own fate that I pretend to be. Don't require me to tell you that I am dependent on you for love and nurture, for a shelter against the cruelty and impersonality of the world. *It castrates me.*"

And yet the barriers to intimacy between husbands and wives are not the "fault" of one sex or the other;

women of our generation, from what I recall of my own life and from what women told me, were as much a party to the separate worlds of men and women as were their husbands. By establishing themselves firmly in a life-style as self-contained as glass domes, they precluded the part of selfhood that would establish common ground between husband and wife. Dr. Robert Seidenberg explains how the mores of our generation reinforced these separate roles:

> There must be a division of work and responsibilities, and this must be responsive to the all-important biological needs served by women. This is to bear and nurture and there can be no adequate substitute for this. . . .
> The male has always been and must be more than a husband or a father. If that is all he aspires to, we know that he is destined to fail, for one can be nothing before there is identity as a person with goals of personal development and achievement. . . . What of the woman? Strangely enough, she may be censured if she aspires to anything more than mother and wife.

Most of the women of my generation did not risk that censure. Their choice was to apply all their energies and interests into the job at hand—occupation: housewife. Marriage, for all the illusion of romance, was an "arrangement" that was backdrop to the rest of one's life goals. For the wife, it was, of course, the rearing of a family; for a husband, his work. Parenthetically, as recently as three years ago, I was interested to observe at a Life Planning session given by the pioneer foundation for behavioral science, National Training Laboratories, that each of the men in my group, when asked to define himself in ten words, headed his list with his professional title—physician, engineer, and so on. Not one used the description "husband" anywhere in his list (all were married) although several listed "father" as one of their personae. Every woman, with only one exception, headed her list with the word "wife," followed usually by "mother"—although most were professionals or businesswomen. Not only the vocational identity, but the sense of personhood was missing entirely from the women's lists.

Speaking to a marriage counselor in preparation for this chapter, I asked him to tell me what it was that made communication between husbands and wives so difficult. It was his view that much of it had to do with women's own vision of themselves. "I recently asked one couple," he explained, "to tell me what each saw about himself as lovable. The wife began by telling me that she thought she was deserving of love because she was a good housekeeper, a good cook, a good mother, that she did a lot of things for her family, that she put them first. The husband, on the other hand, thought he was lovable because he saw himself as a kindly person, with a good sense of humor, a lively imagination. She was stunned when he told her that the reason he cared for her was because of her *qualities*, her warmth, her common sense. She perceived herself only as an object of service. Well, it's hard to relate to an object of service."

How far apart the "separate but equal" roles can take us during the course of a marriage was unfolded graphically and tragically in the in-depth television study, *An American Family*, WNET's documentary about the William Loud family of Santa Barbara, in

1971. Originally selected because they were a "typical" family, successful in the American way—a
handsome couple with all the accouterments of
success, a thriving business, a ranch house with a
swimming pool, five children—the Louds ultimately
present to the viewer the vision of a marriage into
which each of the partners had retreated behind a wall
of noncommunication, of emptiness and alienation.
Ultimately, we watch Pat ask Bill for a divorce, but the
breakdown of the marriage, perhaps accelerated under
the relentless probing of the television camera, is
rooted in the divergent ways in which they have gone
during the years in which they were "together."

The dissolution of the marriage is marked not by
angry fights, but a slow attrition; it ends not with a
bang but with a whimper. Writing to his son Lance,
Bill reflects on the breakup of his marriage:

. . . Your mother is the most difficult to forsake.
She is truly the only person I ever really loved with
my entire heart and soul. She is a completely honest
woman, with an honesty that makes her very
beautiful to me. She has been my Rock of Gibraltar,
both as a snug harbor of security and also as a
perilous navigation hazard for 20 years. At the same
time, and I guess its the famous "American social
custom," marriage requires 100 percent attention
and devotion to duty, a living style of "all or nothing
at all."

Writing about the family in a perceptive article in
the *New York Times Magazine*, February 18, 1973,
Anne Roiphe presents an interpretation of Bill's
problems:

Bill attributes the breakup of his marriage to the forced togetherness of American life. Many, many men are unfaithful to their wives, and many unhappy women, feeling insecure, rejected sexually, sad and unlovable, like Pat Loud, leave their husbands in hope of something better. . . . We women struggle to find a sense of worth, dignity and self-sufficiency, and to create some joy, and possibly, for some, a new love. But men seem burdened by the children, by their career disappointments, by their own ghosts of past pain and future terror. Many American men will sympathize with Bill Loud's dilemma because he needs love, needs his children, needs roots and home and support and warmth, and at the same time needs quiet, the kind teen-age children don't give him, needs adventure, personal expression, conquest, fulfillment beyond the marriage bed. When we see Bill on camera talking with the strip miners out on the road, he looks his best, charming, relaxed, masculine in the old-fashioned way . . . he seems happier without the daily conflict and defeat of family life. It's understandable that he should want to go on a long trip and perhaps never come back.

Pat, on camera, in a moving monologue explaining the divorce to her brother and sister-in-law, speaks for herself:

In twenty-one years we never had a relationship where we could really understand each other. We could talk for hours about anything that wasn't personal. Sex is just a courtesy. . . . Thank you Ma'am. I have no sex life; I'm too young for that.

Now he's getting more careless about leaving lipstick and powder on his shirts. . . . Maybe he

wants me to know so I'll stop him, but I can't. . . .
He scares me. I don't understand all that moodi-
ness. . . . I feel now all our good family times were
not real . . . that we were only a little part of his
life.

The Louds' marriage broke up after twenty years, a
time that is not marked on statistical tables as the most
likely time for a divorce but, nevertheless, the period
that Dr. Jesse Bernard finds to be the lowest time in
marital happiness. Following Dr. Bernard's findings,
in which she divides the phases of marriage according
to the ages of the children—a device I found was
logical since most women automatically use the same
method of demarcation—the early years of marriage
("Pre-Child" according to Dr. Bernard) were the
happiest: "General marital satisfaction, high; positive
daily companionship, high." It is in the next phase, in
which the children are preschool age and of school age
that the picture begins to change, as each partner goes
firmly into his separate world of endeavor. Marital
satisfaction plunges and remains low; in fact, it is at its
lowest ebb during the years that the children are
adolescent—or chronologically, the time in which
most women enter their middle years.

The stresses and strains that come into marriage
specifically at this time were reviewed in an earlier
chapter as part of the general picture of the jumping off
into the middle years; they bear no repeating. It is
again a cliche to say that marital happiness is related to
satisfaction in all other phases of life; the equation is
somewhat useless, for it turns out to be something like
this: "Happy people are happily married." Yet my
questions when I spoke to women about their own

marriages at this time tended to emphasize positive
answers, not because I wished to be Pollyanna about
marriage, but rather because *in spite of all the
problems inherent in the situation, most women of our
generation marry, stay married, prefer to be married,
and by and large see no viable alternative to marriage.*
The questions, then, to which I sought answers were:
How do you view marriage at this time in your life?
How do you deal with the negotiations necessary to
the sustainment of the union? What does your
marriage offer you now, and what sacrifices does it
require from you? How has your marriage evolved
through the years, and what do you see in the future?
In brief, I asked women how *their* marriages worked
for *them*.

Among the women with whom I spoke there were
wide ranges in responses. I spoke with women who
saw their marriages only as the lesser of two evils: "If I
were financially secure, I wouldn't stay with him" or,
"The alternative—being alone—is worse." I interviewed women who spoke about a sort of "peaceful
coexistence"—"As time goes on, he goes more his way,
and I, mine." But I heard from women whose
comments were positive too: "For all the differences
between us, he's my best friend." And even: "I
couldn't imagine my life without him." The single
point on which all the women agreed was something
like this: "I consider marriage the most demanding
aspect of my life, requiring of me all of my resources,
constant adjustments and negotiations, and most of
all—*compromise.*"

It was the word "compromise," in fact, that was the
key. The women who seemed to have the most
workable marriages were those who had abandoned an

absolute vision of marriage—the child's view of a romantic liaison that included complete congruence between the partners. The compromises these women made included not only adjustments on a daily level—negotiations regarding finances and recreation, choice of friends, and relationships with family—but emotional compromise as well. One woman in her late fifties who considered her marriage reasonably successful, put it this way: "A few weeks ago I thought that everything had piled in at me at once, and I plunged into a real depression. When I turned to my husband for comfort, he got angry. He told me that I take things too seriously, and that sort of thing. It occurred to me that throughout our marriage *I* had been the nurturer, that I was expected to be sympathetic to his problems, while his response to mine was annoyance. Then I realized that this was one of those areas that he couldn't manage, but that somehow I had learned to live with years ago. My way of handling depression is to retreat—go upstairs and lie down with a book. It's worked for me, more or less for years, and even though I would *like* more support from him, I suppose I've learned not to expect what he can't give, just as I suppose he's learned to compromise on some of the things he expects from me."

To some of the women the word "compromise" also meant a conscious intermingling of roles. They had undertaken to bridge the chasm that had grown between them as a result of the division of labor that had been part of the housewife and breadwinner roles to which they had rigidly adhered earlier in their marriages. Several had found that with the children grown they had been able to share their husband's work; one interviewee spent a few hours a week in her husband's office, helping with payroll; another, a doctor's wife had begun to assist him with routine office work. Interviewing my neighbor—a college professor married to an accountant, who has an enviably happy marriage—on a Sunday afternoon, I was invited to stay for "smorgasbord dinner": an array of cold fish and vegetables which *he* prepared while she and I talked. Conversely, the word "compromise" meant something else to some of the women I interviewed—the granting to their husbands and the taking for themselves the right of privacy. "I sprang the trap I created for myself," one member of my consciousness-raising group explained. "I get a night out now, and I'm not so resentful when he spends time away from me."

A corollary of the ability to compromise was the ability to *tolerate*. Many women spoke about "fighting less as time goes on." Some of them related this to an easier acceptance not only of the partner, but of themselves as well. "Marriage is the place that you do most of your testing. As I've matured, I've put myself on the block less; I found that as I eased up on expectations about myself, I stopped judging my husband so harshly." The word "trust" figures in the discussion: "We've gone through so much together that I've finally begun to believe that our marriage is really going to endure. I don't see each new crisis as insurmountable anymore."

And finally, what I learned from the women with whom I spoke was that many of them felt—in this one area, at least—that time was not the enemy; rather, it is an ally. Reviewing the findings of experts, I saw that it is the fourth decade in our lives that represents the nadir in marital happiness. If we get through the turbulent forties, we can expect an upswing in "general happiness" and "positive companionship" as our children establish lives of their own and our husbands look forward to retirement. We enter the era with the end to rigid role assignments; there is a chance for the establishment of real intimacy when the divergent paths of men and women come together and the "separate worlds" that constitute marriage at last begin to converge.

Chapter 7

ALONE IN NOAH'S ARK

*We are moving from a couple-oriented society, where there is
discrimination against the single, older person who has lost
social status. As women begin to realize their potential and their
rights—not just as appendages—society will see them differently, too.*

— REBECCA ZIMMERMAN, counselor at the Widows
Consultation Center, New York

The vast majority of us—women in the middle
years—have opted for marriage. In a society in which
women are defined by their relationships to men, a
woman without a husband is outside the mainstream
of community patterns and mores. The woman alone
carries with her the stigma of failure; through her
inability to select, attract, or hold a man, she has
placed herself in a position of vulnerability. The
nuclear family makes no arrangements for the woman
without a man—either in terms of living arrangements
or in emotional support. Our family structure cannot
accommodate an "extra" woman. "My mother-in-law
lives with us" evokes a vision of a burdensome
hanger-on; the single aunt or cousin no longer fills any
domestic need in the home as an assistant housekeeper
or unpaid companion. As it is a grudging act of mercy
to house a mother or mother-in-law, it is an admission
of financial or emotional inadequacy to be housed by
her. "We live with mother" means that we are unable
either to cut the silver cord or to pay the mortgage by
ourselves.

Because our society draws the equation "unmarried = alone," we fear the possibility of being without husbands. As girls we question ourselves: Are we "too choosy"? Married, we worry about our husband's health; avidly and fearfully we read articles about how we can prolong their lives. The presence of the divorcée in our crowd is an ominous signal—it can happen to us. We see women without men, sitting in restaurants alone or in pairs or groups; in contrast even a woman dining in sullen silence with a man seems protected, cared for.

But in spite of the fact that we may not select to be unmarried, may in fact sacrifice every other goal to the attainment and sustainment of marriage, the possibility that at some time in our lives we *will* be alone is very real. We tend to marry men somewhat older than we, and their seniority plus higher mortality rates mean that on an average we may expect some eleven years of widowhood. Divorce rates have fluctuated during the past two decades, but nevertheless, they show an overall steady rise, and the largest increase during the past decade has been among marriages of more than twenty years.

As women without men, we fall into three separate groups: widows, divorcées, and those who have never married. To some extent, our situations are not analogous. For the widow there is the pain of bereavement, the regrets—"Perhaps there was something I could have *done*" or, "If only I had. . . ." For the divorcée there is another kind of pain, the sense of failure at having been unable to make the marriage worthwhile and satsifying enough for her husband or herself. And for the single woman, still another kind of deprivation, the feeling of loss in having been, through one circumstance or another, denied what society regards as woman's most fulfilling experiences—marriage and motherhood. But the common thread that runs through the lives of all of us is that we must cope with our problems in a society in which neither social custom, family patterns, employment opportunities, nor even recreational facilities accommodate the special needs of women alone.

Dwarfing all the other roadblocks that stand between the woman alone and the attainment of fulfillment and security is the basic problem of having enough money on which to live. There are two myths to which nearly everyone subscribes; one is that widows own the wealth of the nation, and the second is that alimony is a bonanza for divorcées. Neither is remotely true. The fact is that in 1966 there were fewer than 90,000 women in America with independent incomes of $10,000 a year or more—some one-tenth of 1 percent of all the women over age fourteen. The vast majority of single women work for a living, and older women are on the bottom of the pay scale. *Aging women without men constitute the single most economically deprived segment of our population.*

The financial problems of women alone stem partly from the fact that, as Morton Hunt wrote, our society is unprepared for us; our problem is "a new one in history, no one has thought much about, or yet done any intelligent planning toward that end." In a country in which there are presently 10,000,000 widows, everyone still believes that men and women share longevity patterns. "If something *should* happen to you, you would want your wife and family to be provided for," insurance agents are instructed to tell their male clients; the possibility that a wife will outlive the husband is somehow considered as remote as the odds on being struck by lightning. In a society in which divorce rates are spiraling it is still assumed that every woman marries for life. But it goes deeper than that. Not only does our society still hold onto demographic patterns and mores that have not obtained in more than seventy years—in 1900 mortality rates of men and women were exactly the same, and. divorce was virtually unknown—but *we ourselves* are unprepared for being alone.

Beginning first with society's provisions for the economic realities of widowhood and divorce: Social Security does not cover housewives. The woman who spends her working years rearing a family accumulates no benefits toward pension whatsoever; it is only her husband's income that provides Social Security benefits. Although Social Security taxes are paid out of joint income, upon retirement men receive full pension, but their widows only receive part, as this letter explains:

> I'm the average, typical middle-class widow to whom the Social Security law is very unfair. . . . We have some small savings which we are compelled to use up in order to exist. Our Social Security check is only 82½% of what our husbands would have been entitled to, and that is the problem. . . . Before my husband passed away, I received Social Security on my own. He got a pension from his union and also his Social Security check. That wasn't too bad—we managed to get along. Now at my age all I get is $154.80. This is where the law is unfair.

The real kicker, however, is not that a widow

collecting her husband's Social Security pension encounters discrimination. It's far worse than that. The Social Security office defines a "widow" as a "woman at least 60 years old with no children under her care." A younger woman is classified as a "widowed mother" *if* she has minor children (and is therefore entitled to benefits), but *a widow with no minor children cannot collect any benefits before age sixty unless she is at least age fifty and entirely disabled.* What has happened to the money—again, paid out of joint income—that has gone into her husband's Social Security is a moot point. The fact remains that whereas the society at large prefers to *ignore* the presence of widows among us, the United States government goes a step further. It *obliterates* them.

Most couples, of course, do not rely on Social Security benefits or pension plans to cover the loss of income that comes with the husband's death. Life insurance is designed—ostensibly—to fill the gap in earning between the time of the wage earner's death and the day when the widow becomes eligible for Social Security benefits. But the problem is that most insurance plans turn out to be inadequate to maintain the widow's needs. Again, there are two contributing factors: the practices of the companies themselves and women's own attitudes. Bernice Malamud, a Long Island insurance agent whose special concern is the needs of women, told me, "I spend a good deal of time with widows trying to help them in making decisions about the options open to them under their husband's policies. So many times there is just so little money! I've asked women why—when I can see that their homes show that their circumstances *were* comfortable—they have been so inadequately provided for. The answer is always the same: 'My husband took care of everything. I never asked him anything—and I wish now that I had.'"

Insurance companies "use women as tools to promote insurance," Ms. Malamud explained. "When you look at the ads, you see a man surrounded by his wife and children and a message that goes something like this: 'Are you caring for the needs of those you love?' But when it actually comes down to sales, agents are more interested in commissions than in widow's benefits, and the highest commissions are given for the sale of whole life policies where the premiums are high, rather than term insurance. That means that most men cannot really afford enough insurance for their families' needs, and they are not sold plans that actually would protect their wives."

Women are not protected under inheritance laws. The first of the cruel financial realities of widowhood comes immediately with the husband's death; most of the assets, unless provision has been made in advance, may not be available until the estate is settled. A widow actually may have to borrow money for funeral expenses. Probate may tie the estate up for endless months; in addition to all the sorrows connected with death, widows are faced with the intricacies of litigation. Furthermore, in some states, if a woman has not "materially contributed to the family's income" (homemaking is, by the way, *im*material!), she must pay an inheritance tax on her "husband's estate"— including, of course, the very home she has cared for all those years!

Nor are widows likely to benefit under their husband's company pension plans. William V. Shannon explains in the New York *Times* of September 9, 1973:

> Since women tend to outlive men, widowhood is a predictable event. Yet virtually all plans either make no provision for widows or require the husband to choose a lower pension in order to provide his survivors with any benefit, and that pitifully small. Significantly, only 2 percent of widows collect a private pension. So-called joint and survivor options are no solution to this problem. A widow should be entitled to 50 percent of her husband's full pension as a matter of law.

As of now, however, the reforms pending in pension plans make no better provision for widows than before; Shannon calls the 1973 Senate Finance Committee's bill "feeble" and says that it is "typical of the thinking behind the bill that it writes in generous tax deductions for self-employed persons—lawyers, doctors, architects . . . who have individual pension plans . . . the very workers who are least in need of Congressional protection" while denying it where financial reform is most needed.

But if our legal system is no friend to the widow, it is perhaps even less fair to the divorcée. Only eight states have community property laws, which means that the vast majority of American women do not necessarily legally own any part of the assets that have been acquired during their marriages! In lieu of division of property, alimony is offered—"support . . . at the *discretion* of the court" according to Webster's unabridged dictionary. But alimony not only is not mandatory, but is generally not awarded and is rarely, if awarded, collected. Statistics show that only 49 percent of the husbands whom the courts have assessed for alimony pay at all. According to William Goode in a comprehensive study, *After Divorce,* the divorced woman "receives relatively little property from the split of joint possessions, is given very little child support, and in two-fifths of the cases does not receive this support regularly." Courts are reluctant or unable to enforce collection, alimony laws do not pertain if the husband leaves the state, and when husbands default, the adversary system of justice requires constant and expensive litigation that discourages women from pressing their legitimate claims.

The combination of legal discrimination, inadequate government planning, and corporation indifference and greed almost inevitably places the woman alone in a financial bracket much lower than that of her married sisters. A husband, as Patricia O'Brien points out in *The Woman Alone,* is "security. He means groceries in the cupboard and shoes in the closet." But compounding our difficulties is our own inability or reluctance to manage whatever assets are available to us. Investments, annuities, interest, banking, escrow, dividend—the very words convey a world as masculine as the sequence of cigars, bay rum, and billiard rooms. "I don't even know how to write a check," married women whom I interviewed told me, or "Money is my husband's department. I just take care of the household bills." I'm prepared to swear that some years ago in the real estate office where I worked, I took a telephone listing for a house placed on the market by a recently widowed client; she did not know whether the house had a $17,000 mortgage on it, a seventeen-year mortgage, or a mortgage at 17 percent! Confronted with the need to head our own households financially as well as in every other way, we are uncertain, unknowledgeable, and moreover, we are not taken seriously by others. Widows and divorcees are prey for unscrupulous lawyers and investment counselors; we are accustomed to depending on *men*, and neither our training nor previous experience prepares us for the time when it will be *ourselves* upon whom we will have to depend for financial security.

As we have been directed to turn toward men for support, so have we become accustomed to relying on relationships with men in our needs for love and companionship. The second common thread that runs through the lives of single women is *loneliness*. "I drove out to my summer house to open it for the season," an interviewer explained. On the way out I thought, this is going to be the first year that it will be just the children and me, but when I got there, I put the thought out of my mind, there was so much to do—mice got into the mattresses, the refrigerator was musty, and I worked all day. Then, as I was leaving, I made a mistake backing out of the driveway, I didn't realize that the ground was all mud, and my car slid, jamming my door against the tree. I became terrified, and I thought, 'I'm trapped,' even though I could get out through the other door. Finally the fear subsided enough for me to get out, and then I couldn't remember that I had already had the telephone service turned on. When I did remember, I called the tow truck; I sat on the porch to wait for it, and I realized what the panic was all about. The divorce hit me. I was in trouble, and there was no husband to call. I was alone."

Sometimes the knowledge of aloneness is hidden in

the fog of depression: "I have trouble sleeping. I wake up after four or five hours. I suppose it's finally gotten to me; I'm forty-five, I'm not married, I have no children. I live in an apartment with rented furniture. Nothing belongs to me, and I don't belong to anyone."

Sometimes it is simply a pervasive feeling of emptiness: "There are times when I can't get to bed, can't face the darkness and the quiet. I lie down on the couch with the TV on, and then a few hours later I wake up and tumble into my bed. It gets to me at night."

Sometimes it is expressed in anger: "It's so unfair. We struggled for so many years, and finally everything fell into place. My daughter got married; the business was making more money than we could use. I thought we could finally travel, live the way we wanted to, and then he got sick."

Listening to women talk about their loneliness, I seemed to hear it most poignantly expressed by widows and divorcées. The women who had never married seemed the least lonely—perhaps because they had learned long-term accommodations or because by personality predisposition, they leaned toward solitude and independence. "I'm a reader," a schoolteacher who had never married explained. "When you have a good book, you always have company." The never-married women whom I interviewed all spoke about abiding interests—travel, study, the outdoors. They were accustomed to determining their own fields of endeavor and recreation; they had what seemed to me a stronger sense of independence and self-determination than either widows or divorcées. Unlike the previously married, they had become accustomed to planning their lives without men; their friendships and family ties were built on the fact that they were single—not one-half of a unit.

The readjustment to a social life in which one is "suddenly alone in Noah's Ark," as a friend defined it, was the shared experience I found among both widows and divorcées. There was a common pattern; for a time married friends had made special efforts to include them as part of a threesome—perhaps for Saturday-nights-at-the-movies. "I understood it was charity," a widow told me. "My friends would call me up and tell me to come along with them—to dinner at the Club, maybe—because it was 'better than sitting home alone.' I guess they were all worried that I would brood. But they never said it would be fun for *them* if I came along, and after a while I started to hate it, and I guess they felt they had done their duty. So now I don't see much of them as couples—I see the women or talk to them on the phone, but I've made a separate social life anyway."

All the women with whom I spoke were aware of the fact that a single man is considered an asset at a party, a single woman a hazard. Why? I wondered. The answer I got was unanimous: Married women are threatened by the presence of an unattached female. "They all know it's *their* husband you want," a forthright divorcée told me.

Our culture does not subscribe to the truth that mature women can still be sexually desirable: Joan Crawford's portrait of the heroine of *Autumn Leaves* is poignant rather than devastating; Mrs. Stone's Roman Spring is a debacle; Mrs. Robinson is a hateful old lecher. In contrast, Gary Cooper and Audrey Hepburn were an entirely believable pair; Gable got Monroe (young enough to be his daughter), and Marlon Brando's co-star in *Last Tango in Paris* was a toddler when Brando made the colored lights go on for Vivien Leigh in *Streetcar.*

Constantly faced with the reinforcement of the double standard of aging, mature unmarried women not only are aware that their "marketability" for remarriage diminishes each day, but are made to feel a lack of personal worth. The diminishment of one's ego with age is true for all women in our society, but the single woman, unfortified by the approval of at least one man to whom she is "special," is particularly vulnerable. Moreover, the already difficult problem of solving the dilemma of how to deal with one's sexual needs in a country in which there are three unmarried women at age forty-five for every unmarried man is complicated by women's own low self-image. "Just when a woman reaches the age she feels most tenderly romantic, she often becomes a little self-conscious about her appearance," says the Oil of Olay advertisement. "Little lines and a dry complexion reveal that she isn't as young as she used to be. So she turns the lights down low when the man in her life is present, hoping to preserve the illusion of earlier days and nights." Or, more directly, as in this letter to columnist Ann Landers:

> I can see how middle-aged couples might still be attracted to one another—physically, that is—if they have managed to keep their looks. . . . After four children, I have varicose veins, 20 extra pounds on my hips and I'm a tired-looking old hag. When I see myself in a full-length mirror after a shower I know, too well, that when he makes a pass at me, it means

he is desperate. I have nothing that would turn anybody on.

The double standard of aging is part of the double standard of sexual morality which, too, works to the disadvantage of mature single women. Our patterns of passivity, of waiting to be wooed, the fixed roles that require men to be aggressors, women receptors are a handicap to both social and sexual functioning at this time in our lives. "I can't get used to the idea it's all right for me to call a man," women have told me. "It just isn't something I can do, even though it seems silly for me at this stage in my life to have to wait at the telephone." Women spoke to me about resenting the attitude of men. "They're so independent" was an expression I heard several times. "If I go to a singles gathering, I have to take the initiative in meeting men, and I just can't do that."

Nor does our society make accommodations for single men and women to meet each other. Reading the novels by Isaac Bashevis Singer about life in the *shtetls* of Poland, I was struck by how much a community concern the remarriage of a widow or widower is: The synagogue, matchmakers, friends, and relatives instantly become involved in arranging meetings—an eligible widow is invited to "visit" from another town, while an air of festive anticipation sweeps the village. A match is to be made! And yet in our society, marriage-oriented as any old-world village, often widows and divorcees are required to wait demurely, hoping that perhaps some friend will "dig up" an eligible man. In large cities, such as New York, there are singles clubs advertised in the newspapers, dance classes, cruises, special weekends at nearby resorts. Travel agencies such as Club Mediterranee attract a "single crowd," and local media such as the *Village Voice* publicize a variety of singles activities in which men and women have an opportunity to meet in a respectable and reasonably pleasant way. But in suburbs and small towns often the opportunity for singles is at bars, an option that many women are reluctant to utilize; churches, country clubs, and other social organizations in our society are not geared toward the needs of unmarried adults.

But even more important, perhaps, is the fact that women returning to single life after years of marriage must now cope with the changing morality of our times. Brought up to view chastity as the feminine norm, we find the new morality at once incomprehensible and threatening. We are caught in a double bind: Whereas earlier generations of women were taught that they had no biological or psychological sexual needs—sexual appetites were part of male functioning, not female—we have been made aware that sexual drives are natural to us too, while at the same time we are still caught in the double standard that permits men casual sexual encounters but requires deep emotional commitment from women. Sex without love is empty, meaningless for women, we have been told, and we tend to believe it. A variety of sexual experience has been traditionally available to men and denied to women—or at least "good women" or "emotionally healthy women." It is not just that we risk censure in seeking sexual contact that is not sanctioned by either marriage or, at the very least, romantic love and fidelity—"the neighbors will talk." We have been told that such behavior is unsatisfying and unfulfilling.

The double standard of sexual morality limits all our relationships with men. If being "free" and "on the town" evokes the vision of a carefree bachelor, it connotes no such idea about a woman. A single woman who is uncommitted to one man is never assumed to be enjoying her freedom; she is marking time until Mr. Right comes along. A date with a man who is less than eligible—not of the right age, religion, financial standing—is not a "fling" for a woman; it's a make-do accommodation to being manless. Women are therefore required to restrict their social lives to men whom a conscientious matchmaker or ambitious mother would approve as a prospective husband. "There's no point in my *wasting time* with a man I couldn't be serious about," I heard from a forty-five-year-old widow, who in fact has since married a sixty-year-old man whom she had known before his divorce.

The double standard pertains to our ambiguous situation in our roles as mothers and as former wives. We are at the same time lonely and denied privacy; as single women we are somehow bound to maintain the morality of marriage. If our children are grown, it is understood that our homes are always available to them; while *their* apartments may be "pads" in which they can entertain or be alone at will, *we* are expected to welcome surprise visits. "How can I tell my son that I wish he would not just drop in on me—that I might be entertaining a man for dinner, or whatever, and not want company? He still sees me as home with an apron on." Another, a friend who has a grown daughter who is openly involved in a sexual affair with a young man she is thinking about marrying, told me that she concealed the fact that she was sexually active too. Why, I asked her, if her daughter could tell her honestly that she was spending the night at her boyfriend's apartment, did she have to lie about the nights that she spent at *her* lover's home ("I'll be at Aunt Audrey's tonight")? "Oh, I don't know," she said ruefully. "I just can't get past the idea that I'm the *mother*." Only one woman told me that she had leveled honestly with her sixteen-year-old son. "He has to get used to the idea, sooner or later, that his father and I are divorced and that I am now free to make my own life. If I go away with a man for the weekend, I'm damned if I'm going to say that I'm spending it with a sick friend. I told him I'll always be a mother, but I'm no longer a wife. He needs to know that women are people too."

If the double standard restricts women in their social behavior with men, it is equally effective in deterring us from alternative relationships—friendships with women. One can "sit home" or go out with a *man*; it is socially outre to go out with "the girls." A group of men in a restaurant are assumed to be enjoying each other's company; a "night out with the boys" is a respected male tradition. A group of women dining or going to the theater are castoffs, pooling their company to avoid loneliness. Women are, after all, second-class; to choose to associate with them is to reveal your own inadequacies. My sister-in-law, niece, and I, after a delightfully close, companionable day together, decided to dine out; the hostess at the restaurant we chose (which, incidentally, is owned by a woman) counted us as we walked in. "Are you ladies *alone*?" she asked, and looked baffled when we protested. Women are *not* alone only when they are escorted by *men*.

Single women socializing with other women are aware of both discrimination and poor public image. "It's just understood that a group of women don't rate the same choice tables that couples or groups of men do. I'm tired of sitting near the kitchen dodging the swinging door." "I've never figured out what you do to get the waiter's attention when you're not with a man. Or to get a cab, either. I tip as well as a man does, but I'm caught in the stereotype anyway." "I feel self-conscious when I'm out with another woman." Women alone or with other women never seem to be doing it out of choice. "I think everyone is saying, 'poor thing,' and I make a spectacle of myself to prove to other people that I'm really having a *wonderful* time."

One of the solutions to the problem of maintaining a full social life without a husband to serve as escort or dinner partner, particularly in large cities and among businesswomen for whom public appearances are a necessity, is the pairing of male homosexuals and mature women. "I meet a lot of gay men in my business, and we get along very well," an attractive divorcee who is a retailing executive told me. "We have a lot in common; even though we've made it in the business world, we're on the outside socially. I have a gay friend—we fill each other's needs. We can appear as a 'couple' in situations where I need an escort, or he needs a date, and there are things that we like to do together, on our own. When I get lonely, I can call him up and say, 'How about a movie tonight?'" Another woman, a designer, shared her cottage at the seashore with a homosexual friend one summer. "It was great," she told me. "There were all the advantages of a housemate—we shared expenses—

and none of the hassles. We gave each other plenty of privacy, and we got along fine on basic issues like who did the cooking and how the place was to be maintained."

Besides being available—"eligible men are scarce as hen's teeth, but there are plenty of gays"—homosexual men are "less demanding, more sensitive, and better looking." Women told me that their friendships with gay men were rewarding because homosexuals appreciate maturity in a woman: "They're not looking for a pretty face. They want a woman who understands them as people and who is discreet and nonjudgmental." Then, too, women feel they can be themselves with homosexual men: "Gays don't feel threatened by independent women." The pop art heroines in the gay world are not sex kittens; they are earthy, forthright, individualistic females: Mae West, Bette Davis, Bette Midler.

Our society is still locked into the vision of Noah's Ark as a travel vehicle, in spite of the fact (although I could find no statistics to prove my point) that single women are probably the largest group of people who travel for recreation. Airlines and hotels are evidently the last to know. "I called for airline reservations," a friend complained. "I was told that there are special rates for couples—but the 'couple' is husband-and-wife. It's a hundred and forty-nine dollars for him, and a hundred an twenty-one for me to go to Florida. 'Suppose I go with another woman,' I asked. Why, then, we both go full fare. What are the airlines doing—pushing marriage?" "One of the things that I've become conscious of," one woman told me surprisingly, "is how *un*-sexist America is. I'd definitely advise any woman *not* to go to the Orient without a

man. You might as well have two heads as be
unescorted in Japan." But more typically, I heard
women complain about the difficulties encountered in
making arrangements through travel agencies: "I had
made plans for a trip to Yugoslavia, and it never
occurred to me that the only way a woman can go is as
part of a double occupancy. I called the agent, the
airlines, I raised every bit of hell I could, but all to no
avail. What I finally realized is that the only way I can
travel on a tour is with another woman."

A number of women made similar observations:
"On any group travel plan or tour, I have no choice; I
must room with a stranger. Women are not allowed to
go places *alone.*" At resorts, too, the situation is
intensely discriminatory; a lovely hotel I visited in the
White Mountains had a "small number of single rooms
for men" but no accommodations whatsoever for
women choosing to room alone.

Noah's Ark is a domicile, too. Many women spoke of
the difficulties of dealing with everyday household
matters without a man. They felt they were overcharged by mechanics, appliance repairmen, painters,
and plumbers. One woman described an experience
with a contractor who had installed a dog run. "He
asked me several times where my husband thought it
should be placed. I told him *I* was taking care of it,
whereupon he promptly overcharged me eighty
dollars. I found out by calling under a different name
and getting an estimate. I've stopped the check; I
expect a lot of trouble, but I'm tired of being cheated
because I'm a woman."

Women also spoke of the difficulties of getting credit
cards and charge accounts. One woman, newly
separated, called the telephone company to request

that the phone be listed under her name. A telephone representative called her back and inquired whether there had been a "divorce or separation." "I was furious and told her that it was none of her business. But it turned out it was; she was going to get a deposit out of me—I had no credit rating, if you please, because the phone had been in my *husband's* name. I told her if she tried that, I'd bring suit, and she backed down. But how about the woman who get easily intimidated? They pay through the nose!"

For women who had until recently shared their homes with husbands, the difficulties of being both housewife and "househusband" loom largest. "It's rough to live alone in the suburbs," one told me. "I can't get repairmen, I don't know how to fix anything myself. I've finally learned how to change a fuse, but I can't do anything else. As soon as my daughter goes off to college I'm going to take an apartment in the city. Let the superintendent take care of things." I was reminded of how effective is the conditioning that tells women they are not mechanical; one woman who had never married had recently bought a small summer cottage that she was converting into a retirement home against the day, soon to come, when she would give up her job and city apartment. "I like to paint, I can even do wiring and a little basic plumbing, but boy, do the neighbors think I'm a freak when I get out there in overalls and nail down loose boards in the deck!" she told me with wry amusement.

Entertaining, too, was a source of concern. I thought about an acquaintance of mine who had recently married a man she had known for many years and whose marriage to his "child-wife" had been desperately unhappy. "When he told her he thought they would be better off apart, the first thing she said was, 'But how am I going to give dinner parties?'" I had laughed ruefully when I heard the story, but speaking with women who were recently divorced, I heard the same fears expressed. Only a few women told me that they found living alone an asset in entertaining: "I don't have to have formal parties anymore," one said. "People make allowances—I can invite some friends over for spaghetti or chili, and I like it much better this way."

A consistent thorn in the sides of most women alone was the difficulty around holidays and special events. "The first Thanksgiving that I was alone I spent all day in bed weeping," a divorcee told me. "I thought about the years past when I had all my family around me. That year the kids went to my mother-in-law's, and naturally I wasn't invited—and wouldn't have gone if I had been." Other women spoke of being lonely at Christmas and New Year's. "If I'm single forever, I'll never get used to going through the holidays alone." Mother's Day was another wrench; a few women told me they had just made up their minds that holidays were "days like any others" and refused to allow themselves to sentimentalize, but for most, holidays were met with some feelings of loneliness and regret.

Compiling the material for this section of the book from personal interviews, research material, notes taken during consultations with specialists, there were times when it seemed to me that being alone is an unalloyed tragedy. For some of the women with whom I spoke, it was. There was certainly no sidestepping the grief of mourning for the widow—the shattering silence of an empty house, the void of the now unoccupied chair at the breakfast table, the fact that, as Diana Horowitz, director of the Widows Consultation Center in New York, explains, "few understand the problems and expect women to recover very quickly from the loss of a husband, but bereavement has no timetable." Nor is there any denying the anger and resentment of divorce, the guilt and feeling of failure toward the children whose homes were no longer intact. But for all that, there were women—and not a few of them—who had found workable solutions to some of the problems of being single and had learned simply to endure those for which there were no answers. For some women being single was, in fact, a life situation that offered its own rewards—freedom, self-development, self-reliance.

Freedom was defined in a number of ways. For some it was personal indulgence. "I can arrange my time the way I want it. I don't have to account to anyone for what I do with my money; it's mine to spend as I like, even if I have less than I did." It was an opportunity to develop their own interests. "He didn't like concerts or the theater, and so we rarely went. This year a friend and I are alternating on a season ticket to the opera, and I really enjoy it." It was a chance to express their own social preferences: "When we separated, I dropped 'the crowd' and made my own friends. I can spend time now with people I really like, not the ones whom I 'owe' a return invitation!" Travel was high on the list. No longer tied down to a husband's schedule, some women were free for the first time to fulfill lifelong desires to see new places, find new experiences.

Self-development was the second of the compensations of being single. "If I had stayed with my husband," a woman in my consciousness-raising group told me, "my life would have been easier in many respects, but I would not have had the chance to *grow*." Reviewing her own life in the past few years, she found it fulfilling, exciting; she had risen through the ranks in her labor union to become president of the division, returned to college at night and received an Associate of Arts degree in labor relations, and now was part of a specially selected group enrolled for leadership training at Sarah Lawrence College. With a new career in the offering and a thirty-year-old yearning for higher education satisfied, she had few regrets about her life.

And finally, at the highest level, there was the opportunity for personhood, for full self-reliance. Describing her experience in recognizing the strengths that her clients possess and helping them use "those qualities of strength as building blocks until the ego is restored," Rebecca Zimmerman, a counselor at the Widows Consultation Center, concludes that "the death of a husband is not the source of being overwhelmed. Rather, their strengths in crisis were never developed enough. Women are not encouraged to reserve a quantum of independence, to know they can rely on *themselves*." Once alone, women do find—sometimes in unexpected ways—that they have untapped resources, capacities for survival, potential for what Patricia O'Brien describes as a "separate psychic existence which involves taking primary responsibility for one's own emotions and adjustments to life." There is then the possibility for true security or, in the words of one of the women I interviewed, "the chance to find out that I can take care of myself, that I can be my own best friend." It is this confrontation with oneself that women alone must face or retreat to the isolation that our society assigns to all women without men.

Chapter 8

THE WORKING WOMAN

After a decade of striking change, the American woman is now considerably more likely to attend college, work, live alone, marry late, be divorced or separated, and outlive her husband than she was at the start of the nineteen-sixties. . . . The proportion of married women in the labor force rose . . . from a quarter to a third. . . . This is largely accounted for by soaring numbers of women 35 to 45 years old who return to work after their children start growing up.
        —News item, New York *Times*, April 10, 1973

In the end the problem remains empirical: not whether women should work, but how those who want to, or need to, can work without leaving their other obligations unsatisfied . . . if society assumes implicitly that women shouldn't work because their place is at home, and regards women who do work as flying in the face of custom or even nature, then there is no need for society to do anything to help them . . . the effort to change customs and institutions may lag very considerably because of the mythic residue at the bottom of our minds. . . . It encourages, by complacency, that effective method of heading off any push for change by assuring the world that the change has already taken place, that women have all the rights they need, or at least as much as is good for them and for their families.
        —ELIZABETH JANEWAY, *Man's World, Woman's Place*

Seated in a circle in a comfortable living room in suburban New York, the eleven women who constituted my consciousness-raising group were a mini-sample of working women in our age bracket.

"I didn't have enough to do, with the children out of the house now, and besides, I got tired of being the only woman in my crowd who didn't have a job."

[161]

Another: "I went back to college and got my degree twelve years ago, when I married my second husband. He wasn't earning enough to support both sets of our children, and we needed another income."

A third: "I began to work when I first came to this country, when I was nineteen. Then, when I had my son, I stayed home with him until he was four, but when my husband left us, I had to go back to work. I've never stopped. I've always been able to make enough to care for us, even when times were hard."

And finally: "I got restless being at home when the children were in school. I wanted to be with stimulating people, in the world of ideas. I wanted to be in an atmosphere where people talk about something besides the Cub Scouts and Little League."

The need may be economic, emotional, intellectual, or a combination of all three. But for whatever reason, the fact is that about half of what the U.S. Department of Labor calls "the mature work force"—women between the ages of forty-five and sixty-four—hold paying jobs outside their homes. *For the first time in American history the largest single group of women workers are past forty-five.*

A brief profile of us as workers: Seven out of ten work full time in year-round jobs. Nearly two out of three are married. Most of us work because we need the money. More than half of us hold clerical or service jobs, a category that includes domestic work. About 13 percent are professionals or technicians. Less than 7 percent hold management positions. Our average yearly salary—as year-round full-time workers—is less than $6,000, about half as much as men our age.

More about us: We are the last hired and first fired.

For women between the ages of forty-five and fifty-four the unemployment rates are twice those of men our age. As we grow older, both our salaries and work opportunities decrease. At forty-five to fifty-four, nearly 70 percent of the single women (widowed, divorced, separated, or never marrried) and nearly half the married women are working; during the next ten years the figures will drop to 60 percent and about 35 percent respectively. At age sixty-five, only three out of ten of us will have incomes over $2,000 per year, and only 8 percent will receive over $5,000 a year! In our society, age is a vocational handicap—only 9 percent of all men and women hired in 1972 were over age forty-five—and being female is a vocational handicap. Despite the efforts of the feminist movement to upgrade women's job standing, the differences between men's and women's salaries were greater in 1970 than they were in 1950.

These are the bare facts. What lies behind them is the basic truth that employment standards are geared to the life patterns of men, not women. A man is expected to work *and* marry, but as Charlotte Perkins Gilman pointed out in *Women and Economics,* published in 1898: "All the roles a female is permitted to play derive from her sexual functions." Or, in a more contemporary idiom, as one of the women whom I interviewed for this chapter explained:

"The greatest source of concern to my employers is not my competence. It's my menstrual cycle. Before I married, I had no future with the company because I would marry and become pregnant. When I wanted to return to work after I had my children I was a bad risk because I might become pregnant again. Now that I'm past childbearing age, I'm even less in demand.

I'm risky because everyone knows you can't trust a woman 'going through the change'; they're tuu emotional and hard to get along with. One of these days I'll get a doctor's certificate swearing I haven't had a period in over a year, and then, of course, I'll be over the hill. I'll be too old for the job!'

The theory that "anatomy is destiny"—a woman's "natural" function is childbearing, her "natural" place is in the home, while any other role is either biologically impossible or socially unsuitable—is subscribed to not only by employers (for whom a work force of married women who do not think of themselves as workers and are not taken seriously on the job provides a pool of cheap labor), but by women themselves. Our conditioning by society and our acceptance of our roles begin early in life and are reinforced all through our middle years. As girls we are taught that the real business of life is attracting a husband; our career aspirations rarely go beyond the moment when Mr. Right appears. During our school years, in our vocational training, we are steered by counselors—with our own acquiescence—into choices predicated on the belief that as women we have certain aptitudes and lack others. Logic, judgment, mathematical and mechanical ability are "masculine traits"; they are also the qualifications for professions that are given highest status and pay in a technological society. Nor, apparently, does our life experience eventually persuade us that our self-definitions were inaccurate; every woman in my consciousness-raising group sees herself as disadvantaged mathematically—"I'm not good at figures at all!"—and the fact that they all efficiently manage their household financial affairs, including mortgage and tax payments, escrow accounts, savings, insurance premiums, has not convinced them to the contrary.

When we actually do begin "careers" (women's work is glamorized thus, perhaps to compensate for the fact that it is undervalued and underpaid), we accept the limitations of our "femininity." We know that we may not "compete" with men; we have been taught to believe that *their* needs, both financial and ego-dictated, are greater than ours. We would rather relinquish responsibility and reward than be labeled "aggressive." In her in-depth study *The Woman Executive,* sociologist Margaret Culser gives convincing evidence that even among the most highly placed career women in America, the role conflict remains a constant: Most of the women she studied were afraid of the stigma of "unfemine conduct" and hence not aggressive enough to push their way upward or to handle situations calling for overtly domineering qualities.

We accept ourselves as "hearts," not "minds." In the office we flirt discreetly, make coffee, water the plants. We are most comfortable in the occupations in which personal services duplicate what women do for their own families. "Not unexpectedly," Caroline Bird explains in *Born Female,* "more than 90 percent of all nurses, baby-sitters, household workers, hotel maids, dressmakers, milliners and dietitians are women." We fulfill, most comfortably, the hostess and comforter roles, as explained approvingly by W. M. Kiplinger, at the National Secretaries Association meeting in February, 1967: "Secretaries are marvelous people. They are ornamental and they are useful. They take down what you say and improve upon it. . . . They hold the mad letters until tomorrow. They answer the telephone,

sidetrack the bores . . . they remember the birthdays. . . . They see when you need a haircut."

We squelch our own ambitions, for we accept the
stereotype of successful women as shrews, castrators,
freaks, rather than as women of accomplishment.
(American women admire as role models women who
achieve prominence as *wives* of important men. The
most "admired women in America" in 1972, according
to a woman's magazine poll, were Mrs. Richard Nixon
and Mrs. Billy Graham.) We try to avoid jobs in which
we must work under the supervision of a woman
rather than a man, partly because we think we can
manipulate men through sexual games and partly
because departments headed by women generally
have low status within the firm itself.

We are, finally, unable to resolve the conflict
between "femininity" and success, for to achieve or
even strive for financial reward, prominence, professional success means that we have made it in a man's
world—and lost ourselves as women. "A suburban
neighbor of mine named Gertie came as I was writing
The Feminine Mystique," Betty Friedan recalls.
"'Occupation?' the census taker asked. 'Housewife,' I
said. Gertie, who had cheered me on in my efforts at
writing and selling magazine articles, shook her head
sadly. 'You should take yourself more seriously,' she
said. I hesitated, and then said to the census taker,
'Actually I'm a writer,' But then, of course, I then was,
and still am, like all women in America, no matter
what else we do between 9 and 5, a housewife."

But it is not only that we are subtly forced into a
choice of being what society tells us is either
passive-and-womanly or ambitious-and-masculine but
that we are literally faced with a choice between

fulfilling our emotional and biological needs for family *or* our needs for self-expression in our work. Whatever the statistics are for working mothers, society's institutions work on the assumption that every mother is home, nurturing her young and baking muffins. There is no system of child care, until recently no adequate provision made for maternity leave, our nuclear homes do not provide for alternate parents, and in short, a working mother is faced with the Herculean and often impossible task of rearing her children with no assistance and maintaining a job.

It is barely acceptable even to be a working wife—let alone mother. For women of our generation, there was something subtly "castrating" about working after marriage; it indicated, at the very least, that one's husband could not fulfill his manly role in bringing home the bacon, and as for the emotional effects, Agnes De Mille spells them out in a witty section in her article "Women at Work":

> Preachers, doctors, teachers warn . . . the women's magazines are particularly explicit: if the wife has to work outside the home, she must never let it impinge on her husband's schedule, and if inside the home, she must see that it is finished and put away before he comes back from his own work and she must never for one moment let him think that hers is more important than his, or his interests and hobbies and needs. And for this reason, and because it will be construed as a direct reflection on his virility, she must not earn more money. He will develop ulcers, sinuses, tuberculosis. He will borrow the classic symptom of women's frustration, the bitter, black headache, and though women's magazines do not care to name this, he will add one

of his own, partial or total impotence, which is a
form of suicide. . . . He may in the end leave her.

The unhappy truth that it is virtually impossible for
women within the framework of the mores and
standards of this society to succeed in business or the
professions while still maintaining a satisfying and
fulfilling family life was pointed out in a study by Dr.
Margaret Hennig, a professor of business management
at Simmons College in Boston, who undertook an
in-depth analysis of the lives of about a hundred
women who are in the top echelons of American
business. Her findings were interesting for what they
tell us not only about "women who made it," but
about how punishing are the choices that successful
women must make.

Describing her subjects, Dr. Hennig found them to
be remarkably similar. Each of the women had been
viewed by her family as a "special" child, encouraged
to "male" interests and accomplishments: math,
science, business. In the working world, each became
an administrative assistant, finding the key to success
in her attachment to a man in the company whose
position she later took over.

They had a choice of several work attitudes
. . . they could become masculine, they could
become everybody's buddy; or they could withdraw . . . all chose to withdraw. Their original goal
was to reach middle management, but suddenly at
age 35, they realized they could go higher still, and
were . . . bored. They were not married, their
childrearing years were fast disappearing, and they
experienced an identity crisis that most men go
through, only several years earlier. . . . At this

point, half of the women married older men, usually widowed or divorced and very successful [the others forfeited marriage entirely]. . . . The men didn't feel threatened by their wives' success, but were highly supportive of their wives' desires to move on to upper management. Up until now, these women had had very little opportunity to develop the other non-technical skills necessary for the top jobs, but now they became much more people oriented and skilled in politics and strategy. . . . Any woman with upper-management goals must be prepared to accept a number of situations, to take risks, to live with ambiguity, to stand conflict and deal with it, to be lonely and live with it, to be out front with nowhere to hide, to be self-disciplined, to be different and live with it, and to be the person where the ball stops rolling.

In short, to reach the highest levels in business, the women Dr. Hennig interviewed had to forfeit close personal relationships, friendships with other women, possibly marriage, and nearly certainly children of their own—a set of requirements successful men never have imposed upon them.

Perhaps many of the attitudes and roadblocks that stand between women and employment outside their homes would have long ago broken down, given the realities of an economy in which most women either choose to work or need to work, if it were not for the fact that industry benefits by keeping women in second-class positions, grateful for every opportunity to bring home a paycheck and unlikely to demand much by way of either salary or other benefits because of their own guilt or feelings of inadequacy. At every juncture, the double standard is a real bonanza for employers. The pretty high school or college June grad is shuffled into the typing pool with the understanding that her minuscule salary is no real hardship for her—surely it's her dad's pleasure to buy her pretty things until she is whisked off by a husband. As a working mother she cannot be placed in a "responsible" position because it's understood that her first priorities are going to be toward her family (I have never met any woman who told me she had been interviewed for a job without being asked how old her children were). Employers cope with motherhood in a number of ways, one of them being to channel women workers into part-time work (some 32 percent of all women workers have part-time jobs, as compared with 13 percent of men workers), thus sparing themselves the expenses of paid sick leaves or vacations, sometimes unemployment insurance, and frequently permitting minimum wage rates. Furthermore, by and large part-time work does not qualify as "work experience" by the standards of most personnel departments, thereby permitting the hiring of women workers at a low salary level.

Both women's life patterns and the double standard of aging tie in advantageously with industry's needs for a cheap labor market. Betty Friedan explains in an article in the New York *Times* on March 4, 1973:

I was subpoenaed Christmas Eve, 1966, to testify before a judge in Foley Square, because the airlines were so outraged at our insistence that they were guilty of sex discrimination by forcing stewardesses to resign at age 30 or upon their marriage. (Why, I had wondered, are they going to such lengths?

Surely they don't think men ride the airlines because stewardesses are nubile. And then I realized how much money the airlines saved by firing those pretty stewardesses before they had time to accumulate pay increases, vacation time and pension rights.)

The benefit to business continues all the way through to retirement. "Pension plans entirely paid by the company discriminate against women workers in a more subtle but nonetheless effective way," Caroline Bird writes in *Born Female.*

A typical "non-contributory plan" will vest, or set aside funds for an employee only after he or she has worked for ten years and reached age 40. This sounds fair enough. If a woman stays ten years and is 40 years old, she gets the pension the same as a man. The fact is, of course, that a woman usually doesn't stay long enough to get the pension. When she leaves, the company hires another woman, and uses the money that would have gone to fund a pension for her job. . . . Women workers lose out in much the same way on group life insurance. . . . Many of these policies provide larger benefits for men than for women workers and pay less to widowers than widows. And insurance plans that give higher salaried employees more coverage often allot them additional insurance on the basis of long service, a proviso that discriminates against women workers who have lost their seniority during child-rearing years or even for taking a few weeks off to have a baby.

Putting it all together then—our own limited aspirations, which are made in favor of the choice of "femininity" over "masculinity," the life patterns which our society assigns to women, requiring us to choose between professional success or love and family, and the businesses' policies of placing us in jobs that are both underpaid and uninspiring—it is not surprising that most of the women of our generation worked briefly for a time before we began our families, possibly began to work part time again or (less typically) full time after our children were of school age, thus putting us in what Morton Hunt calls the pattern of "woman's split career." More women work "in middle life . . . than during their youth. The curve hits its first peak at about age nineteen (when 48 percent work), its valley at age 30 (when 35 percent work), and its second peak at 50 (when 49 percent work)." This, by the way, Hunt continues, "is strikingly different from all the curves of female employment prior to 15 years ago; until then, the percentage of women who worked dwindled slowly and steadily from youth toward old age."

The "split career" is, for most of us, the best accommodation to both worlds: the "outside" world of work achievement and financial reward and the personal world of home and family. But the problem is that it carries with it a heavy price. It means leaving a position and a life of the intellect just when one has a good grip on it, remaining at home while others forge on ahead, and then coming back fifteen or twenty years later, without rank, skill, or accomplishments. Furthermore, the time at which we return to work—at the bottom rung of the employment ladder (for the years spent at home not only do not count as credits in business advancement, but may be a handicap, for we have fallen out of touch with technological, scientific, and business advances during the years at home)—

represent the very years in which we are most in need of financial and ego rewards through our work. Ironically, at the time when most men are at the peak of their career achievement, women are relegated to unskilled jobs or jobs far below those held by men with similar educational levels.

In addition to finding that we are not welcomed by employers when we return to work after ten, fifteen, or twenty years spent at home, because we have "grown rusty" or failed to keep up with new trends in the business world, we face an array of new roadblocks to success. We must again confront the *sex* barrier, now compounded by the *age* barrier, and to add to it all, we ourselves have a new set of personal attitudes that we must overcome.

The first hurdle that we as mature women face upon reentering the working world is the need to deal with our own sense of inadequacy, for whatever else its reward may be, homemaking as a career is not *ego*-building. During the years we have spent at home there has been no opportunity to achieve the confidence and poise that obtain from measurable success in the working world. Entering an employment agency or personnel office, we are aware that we have to sell *ourselves*—for all that we have been told that homemaking requires an abundance of valuable skills, the experience in managing one's home finally does not show up tangibly on a vita sheet—and we do not have the experience to do it. One of the women whom I interviewed spoke about her experience in applying for a job at a local medical center: "I told myself when I called for the appointment to be interviewed that *everybody* is nervous looking for a job, and I tried to comfort myself with the thought that it was only my ego at stake if I failed, I'm not in dire straits financially. But when I got there, I found my little pep talk didn't help me much. The girl behind the desk was young enough to be my daughter, and I felt intimidated by her way of looking right through me. I suppose I need to look for a job in a less prestigious office, but I'm the sort of person who is used to being somewhat in the background—I'm not used to putting myself forward."

Caroline Bird warns working women to beware of offices in which the front-desk receptionist looks like a fashion model. It's a clue, she claims, to the priorities of the firm: Where women are valued for their appearance, they are given low rating for efficiency and are kept in dead-end jobs where their chief value is decorative. But usually mature women need no such warning, for where youth and beauty are status symbols, mature women generally are not even hired. As sexism keeps younger women from advancement, it keeps older women *out*.

Dr. William Holub, a research scientist who is a member of the National Organization for Women, has written about the problem of antiwoman discrimination in business. "Men are conditioned to regard female employees as foils," he told me. "A beautiful, young assistant is an ego booster; it's flattering to men to have them around, admiring them. And it's diverting. Sex adds spice to the workday." (In an article in *Medical Economics*, Dr. Holub graphically described office sexism: Female associates are identified thus—"The one with the legs.") "An older woman," Dr. Holub continued, "isn't a sweetheart—she's a mother figure, and men are in awe of her."

The mother image which men establish and subsequently use as a means of categorizing women appears in Doris Lessing's sensitive novel of middle age, *The Summer before the Dark.* Kate Brown, "forty-odd years" old, recently returned to work, deals with both the role she had been hired to fill, "the supplier of some kind of invisible fluid, or emanation, like a queen termite, whose spirit (or some such word—electricity) filled the nest, making a whole of individuals who could have no other connection," and her own adaptation to it:

> This is what women did in families—it was Kate's role in life. And she had performed this function, . . . it was a habit she had got into. She was beginning to see that she could accept a job in this organization, or another like it, for no other reasons than that she was unable to switch herself out of the role of provider of invisible manna, consolation, warmth, "sympathy." . . . She had been set like a machine by twenty odd years of being a wife and a mother.

Kate Brown is perceptive enough to see what her worth is and practical enough to use it for her ends—although not without some feeling of resentment. But she is fortunate, in a sense, to have that opportunity. Often positions are simply not open to mature women because the "emollient" quality Kate Brown offers is not enough to compensate for the fact that an older woman is an authority figure with which male employers frequently cannot cope. This attitude translates differently in office vernacular, as Letty Cottin Pogrebin points out in writing about the employment problems of mature women in the *Ladies' Home Journal:* "An older woman is not told *she* threatens a fragile male ego—she is told that she will 'resent' working for a younger executive. Or she is told she is 'overqualified,' for various jobs because of her previous experience." The word "overqualified," as Pogrebin explains "is frequently an employer's way of saying that you've worked too long to be hired for a low-level job, but you're too old and female to be hired for the job you deserve."

Even for women who have the jobs they deserve— those who have either had continuous careers in which they have achieved seniority or been able to return to work in professional or executive capacities—the problems of sexism are compounded by bias against middle age. Dorothy Tennov, a professor of psychology at the University of Bridgeport, writes about the middle years in an article, "The Seven Ages of the Professional Woman":

> By 40 . . . she achieves the professional status and recognition—if she has been industrious and fortunate—of an inferior and younger male. Her real potential contribution is still not welcomed, she has even learnt not to hear her ideas herself, unless they are put forth by others. At conventions she is no longer "one of the boys," but unless she is on her husband's arm, simply lonely. She has begun to need cronies. The professional woman at 40 is rejected by our Couples Society which does not understand that men and women can be comrades. . . . Thus men have many good reasons for not socializing with female colleagues, they may find themselves obliged to pick up the tab in a restaurant, they become the victim of scandal and gossip, they may fear that the woman's real aim is to capture a mate. But these "reasons" are often mere rationaliza-

tions. Professional men do not wish to waste their time with a woman colleague when it is only the males who wield the political power within the profession through which their own careers can be advanced. As one male put it: "There are things a man can accomplish with a 'phone call (Hello, Charlie, old pal, how's the wife?) that no woman can possibly achieve, not through the writing of a hundred articles and well-thought out letters. She is outside the network of friendly patronage, gentlemen's agreements and outright deals which make our world go round.

Dr. Tennov's account of her own experiences in the academic world are a behind-the-scenes view of some of the attitudes and conditions that contribute to what the Carnegie Commission on Higher Education calls "a dark age for bright women." Reviewing the inequalities in the American educational system, the commission found that although women constitute more than half of all high school graduates and more than 40 percent of college graduates, they were only 24 percent of faculty, 13.4 percent of those holding doctoral degrees, and 8.6 percent of the full professors.
The question of how we, as women in our middle years, can light a candle in this "dark age" has not yet been answered. The New York *Times* recently acknowledged changes in the general employment picture for women, heading its article "More Women Advancing into Key Business Posts" and pointing out that the gains are "largely a result of government pressure and militant feminism." The article cites recent antidiscrimination legislation, chiefly the Office of Economic Opportunity, which since receiving enforcement powers in March, 1972, has filed some

seventy-three lawsuits alleging sex discrimination (among them a settlement with American Telephone and Telegraph for $38,000,000 in back pay and increases to women and minority males). However, on a direct level, the problems that mature women encounter lend themselves for solution less to utilizing government and social resources than their own reserves. We are unlikely at this age to become militant feminists; even the filing of a complaint with the Office of Economic Opportunity against a corporation that discriminates against us is outside our accustomed system of values. Aging in itself is shameful; how many of us are willing to publicly announce that we have been rejected on the grounds of age? ("You only have to say '21 plus"—the women at the Board of Elections in my district explain reassuringly, in advance, to every mature female registrant.) We are certainly not going to turn out in large numbers for militant demonstrations. "Can you see me with a picket sign marching around an office building?" one of my interviewees asked.

Nor are we likely to be much sustained by help from "the sisters," as are younger women; in our age group there is a countermilitancy movement made up of successful women—Midge Decter and Helen Laurenson, for example—who downgrade the efforts of other women: "If I can do it without a whole movement to help me, so can other women." Or more colorfully, from Joan Crawford, who seems to have missed the point of the whole thing: Feminists are dismissed as "poor little things. They always look so unhappy . . . their mouths look so sour, all pulled down at the corners. They've never tried hard enough to be women." The women's movement, which wants to change some of the rules of the game and let in more players, threatens those who are winning under current rules. And then, too, for many, age brings resistance to change because the individual has a longer investment in the traditional ways and may have personal difficulty in changing deeply ingrained habits and beliefs.

What our work situation comes down to finally is the fact that once again what we must do will have its roots within our *own* life experience; given the realities of a society that has not yet caught on to the fact that changing social and economic realities and a lengthening life span for women will be returning ever-increasing numbers of us into the labor market, it is *we* who are going to have to make the accommodations, being realistic about how we can convert our liabilities into assets and appraising how they can be used.

There is at present time a small vanguard of social agencies which are attuned to our needs and offer intelligent and innovative programs. For example, there is the newly organized Life Planning Center, in Huntington Bay, Long Island. Working with research accumulated by NOW, two professors of counselor education in the Graduate School of Education at C.W. Post College have evolved a practical plan to help women determine how they fit into the job market and assist them in equipping themselves for their new roles.

The counselors begin with an appraisal of each candidate's life experience—an autobiography that includes education and work experience, as well as value systems, health and energy levels, and basic abilities. The program—unlike those of the usual vocational guidance agencies and employment agencies—is sensitive to the conflict that women experience in choices between marriage and careers, and part of its approach includes actually bringing in the woman's family to ensure that they understand and will support her reentry into the job arena. Understanding that women have been subjected to conditioning that makes it hard for them to give supervision and possibly to assume responsibility, the counselors both evaluate and strengthen women's abilities in these areas. And then, from a thorough knowledge of the job market, the counselors recommend courses of study, work progression, or apprenticeships to train for specific jobs, giving candidates help with résumé and responses to classified ads and even rehearsals for job interviews.

How widespread programs as comprehensive and thoughtfully conceived as the center's will become remains to be seen. At the present time most women do not have access to this sort of aid but there is hope in the fact that there is a growing awareness among experts—and more important among women themselves—that women's vocational lives are far more complex than men's, that we are products of an environment that discourages success for women. There is now documented evidence that economic and legal discrimination against women actually exists. All this is a long way from the Panglossian world we lived in only a few years ago, which Betty Friedan describes in a recent article—the time when "whole learned journals were devoted to discussion of 'women and their options'" and women were dismissed by being told they "could go to school, work a bit, get married, stay with the children 15 to 20 years, and then go back to school and work—no problems; no need for role conflicts."

Another banner of hope is the fact that the times are with us. As more and more women enter the working force and the women's movement continues to gain acceptance (at the present time half of all American women support "organized efforts to improve women's status") it becomes increasingly likely that women in the middle years will find social approval for success in the working world. With these changes as first steps, there is the possibility that we can work constructively with the kinds of skills we have, utilizing our life experience in ways that bring fulfillment in careers, rather than remain caught in the contradictions both in our society and within ourselves which prevent us from achieving either status or fair reward for our work.

Chapter 9

MIND AND BODY

Our bodies are our gardens, to the which our wills are gardeners. . . .

—Othello, Act I, Scene I

The vote is unanimous. Ask any one of us what she wants above all for herself in the middle years, and to a woman the answer is good health.

On the surface it would seem that the wish is granted; taking us as a group, we share the best of all blessings. As females, from the moment we are born we are more likely to survive than our male contemporaries, and as we grow older, we not only maintain our edge, but gain ground. A quick rundown on the most direct gauge of health—mortality rates: It is not until we reach age sixty-three that our chances of not living through the year are as high as that of the general American population, which includes both sexes and all ages! For every 1,000 of us women between the ages of thirty-five and forty-four, only 2 will not survive the year, and although the figure will double between forty-five and fifty-four and show a sharp incline between fifty-five and sixty-four, when it will reach 1 percent, the figures contrast strikingly with those for male mortality. During the middle years—in this case between forty-five and sixty-five—exactly twice as many women as men will celebrate another birthday.

Looking at the general health statistics in America,

again we are way out front. In nearly every category (except for those diseases that are unique to the female reproductive system) we are generally less likely to become seriously ill than are men, and if we do, our chances of recovery are far better. The major American killer, cardiovascular diseases, strikes three men for every woman. Although our respiratory disease and alcoholism rates are growing, our mortality in each of the categories remains lower than those of men, and even cancer, the prime killer of women, claims more men than women by some 23 percent. Taking pathology indicators as a whole, all the odds are on our living well into solid old age in reasonable health and strength.

And yet the picture is murky: The middle years are not associated with vigorous good health. "A distinguished doctor once told me that if it were not for the psychosomatic illnesses of middle-aged women, doctors' offices would not be nearly so crowded," writes Josephine Lowman in a syndicated column called *Why Grow Old?* The stereotype of the woman in her middle years includes a composite pathology; the very words "menopausal" and "postmenopausal" suggest a host of subsidiary afflictions: headaches and backaches, insomnia, fatigue, depression. The stereotype not only carries weight generally, but tends to be subscribed to by women themselves. Few of us think of ourselves enjoying good health; most of us complain of at least one chronic ailment—migraines, gallbladder, cystitis—or at any rate of being below par in some area of our health.

What is it that accounts for this odd contradiction? Are we malingerers, hypochondriacs; are our ailments taken too seriously—or perhaps too lightly? Or are our complaints a combination of sociological and psychological conditioning by our society and subject to interpretation, diagnosis, and treatment within the framework of popular medical theory in ways that require us to maintain a state of physical malaise and emotional malfunctioning—a condition of perpetual borderline well-being?

The popular view has it that the ailments of women in the middle years are a result of boredom. Josephine Lowman writes:

> Many middle-aged women who have suddenly been relieved of much responsibility find themselves in poor health. In the past they were busy rearing children, taking care of a home and helping their husbands achieve financial security. Then the day comes when their children are gone and they have enough money to take it a little easier. . . . They had looked forward to this time and cannot understand why they are chronically fatigued. . . . More and more we are recognizing the tremendous effect of mental viewpoint on the health of the body. The boredom and feeling of being unneeded which assail many middle-aged women are well-demonstrated phenomena.

The point is undoubtedly well taken; involuntary early retirement has shown a relationship to ill health and higher mortality in men, too. But surveying women's total health picture, one begins to doubt that there is any very abrupt change with the middle years; all the evidence leads to the theory that throughout our lives we were taught to correlate fragile health with feminity and that even during the years in which we *were* busy and useful, we were subtly encouraged toward patterns of physical and emotional weakness.

The training began for us in childhood; we were taught to be careful of our bodies, to live uneasily within them. We were discouraged from active exercise—it was risky and "tomboyish." Moreover, we were warned that the scars of minor accidents would mar our beauty and diminish our marketability as wives; a woman's face, after all, is her fortune. "It wouldn't be so bad if it had happened to my son," a friend told me some years ago when her daughter's chin was scarred as a result of an automobile accident. Ballet lessons, my dancing teacher explained to Mother—in all seriousness—had to be taught *correctly*; otherwise, there was the danger of "bulging muscles." The ideal female body is fine-boned, unmuscled, delicate, requiring special consideration, particularly in the area of the reproductive organs, which are somehow assumed to be precariously attached to the rest of one's body: "Be careful, don't lift anything heavy—your uterus will drop!"

During our time, the menarche was considered a time of particular peril; menstruation precluded not only physical activity, but even bathing. Remember the notes that excused us from gym when we were *unwell*? The prevailing cultural norm (a remnant of primitive taboos against menstruation) establishing the fact that girls not only are inferior physically, but are *particularly* inferior at certain times of the month or at certain times of their lives, sets the stage for the harvest of discrimination we reap in our middle years with menopause—a situation exquisitely illustrated by a position paper written in 1970 by Dr. Edgar Berman, a surgeon who was an adviser to the U.S. State Department. Women, Dr. Berman wrote, are not qualified to make important foreign and domestic policy decisions because monthly "raging hormonal imbalances" affect their ability to make cool decisions. "Genes," Dr. Berman wrote with the kind of blind authority that requires no facts to support a conviction, "are our masters and our fate." Incidentally, there was no retraction when Dr. Estelle Ramey, an endocrinologist and a professor at the Georgetown University School of Medicine, suggested that since the female of the species is hardier and longer-lived than the male, the double standard contributes to "male fraility." "As a child of my culture," Dr. Ramey wrote tartly, "I don't mind . . . the fun and games of being treated like a fragile flower. But as a physiologist working with the unromantic scientific facts of life, I find it hard to delude myself about feminine frailty."

If Dr. Ramey is undeluded, the media are preoccupied with feminine frailty. Women's magazines barrage us with articles about illnesses. Patricia Neal's recovery from stroke and Shirley Temple's mastectomy were glamorous additions to the routine, women's magazine fare: "How One Family Copes with Mental Retardation." Television soap operas are written around the disease-of-the-month, with brain tumors exerting a special fascination for the writers, if not the viewers. "Blindness, paralysis, amnesia, and subdural hematoma (a blood clot under the skin that covers the brain) are as common in Soapland as headaches in everyday life," the authors of *All My Children* explain cheerfully. Amnesia and paralysis are popular afflictions "because they allow for maximum tragic impact, yet enable the victim to keep up his or her end of the conversation. It's hard to sustain audience interest in a leading character who's been comotose for six months. But blind? Easy!"

The media assume that women are preoccupied with disease—not only their own, but the ailments of other members of their families as well. Perhaps the reason is that nursing a sick child or husband is one of the nobler responsibilities of homemaking (as opposed to the steady maintenance of a family's health and welfare by means of the daily duties of cooking), and there *is* a certain kind of cachet in a unique illness; women are allowed very little other distinction.

Illness serves a variety of purposes in our lives. We are nurturers of others, and the only permission we have to nurture and soothe ourselves, to place our own needs at least on par with those of our families, is when we are ill. When my own children were small, I spent the winters periodically sequestered in bed with enormously visible, drippy, throat-rasping colds from which I had to *protect* the rest of my family—"Don't come near me, you'll catch it!" No power on earth could have convinced me that I had a right to take time away from my family, simply to be alone, to read, sleep, think, to give in to my strong need for solitude; the colds, of course, made it imperative that I do just that. It was not until I decided that my sons had their own activities and friends and did not need me around the clock that the colds mysteriously disappeared.

Illness is a socially acceptable way to be selfish. It is a culturally approved way to be feminine; the Victorian lady swooning in her stays is gone, but her image lingers on. It is, of course, routinely used as a way of regulating one's sex life; the old jokes whose punch line is "I can't tonight, I have a headache" find modern echoes. And finally, illness is the only socially approved method by which we can control our own choice of activity. Given the assumption that no woman can fill all the options open—we cannot achieve perfection as cook, chauffeur, cleaning woman, companion, courtesan, community worker, hostess, bookkeeper, nurse, ad infinitum—and the correlative assumption that we are expected to have others— parents, husbands, and children—determine our roles on the basis of their needs rather than ours, specific ailments serve us in selecting our fields of action. By the degree of physical vigor which we display, we determine how we may fill our roles as wives and mothers.

If cultural definitions of feminity and our own accommodation through our behavior and roles contribute to our patterns of physical pathology, the evidence seems even more convincing that these factors play their part in our mental health. Adrienne Rich makes a strong case in her review of a recent book about mental illness in women, *Women and Madness*, by Dr. Phyllis Chesler. Ms. Rich points out that our mental health picture begins with the definition of behavior itself. We are classified—by ourselves and by our society—on the basis of a "male ethic of mental health, based on the invisible and sometimes explicit assumptions of patriarchal society." By psychiatric definition, a "healthy" woman is assumed to differ from a "healthy" man by being "more submissive, less independent, less aggressive, less competitive, more excitable in minor crises, more easily hurt, more emotional, more conceited about appearance, less objective. . . . a bias steam-ironed into women's lives by early training, education, intensive social pressure, and when necessary, punishment."

Listening to the words themselves that describe behavior, we hear them differently according to the sex of the person about whom we speak. "Aggressive" used to define a woman's behavior evokes the image of a harridan with a bulldog jaw and a voice that shatters glass; about a man it means "go-getter," as, for example, "Help Wanted . . . Aggressive man for training as executive."

Our early training tells us that fear and passivity are not only acceptable female behavior, but desirable traits which we are to learn and practice. Being afraid of objects or situations that one rationally knows hold no danger is given plus value for women—travel phobias, for example. "She's afraid to drive on the Thruway," a male friend told me, patting his wife's knee approvingly. "I told her she just needs a little more confidence in herself." The paragon of Victorian femininity, after all, is helpless, house-bound, child-like. Masochism and narcissism, which are considered indications of pathology in men, are "normal" in women. "I'm a doormat for my family," a woman told me with considerable pride. Likewise, a preoccupation with one's appearance—to the very point of obsession—is the epitome of femininity. "I underwent hypnosis," boasts Princess Luciana Pignatelli, an international beauty, "had cell implants, diacutaneous fibrolysis [this *is* as bad as it sounds—a series of small hooked instruments are used to reach under the skin to loosen the fat on hips, thighs, and upper arms], silicone injections, my nose bobbed and my eyelids lifted. . . . If I had one hundred beauty operations that did not show, that would be all right. It is the way that you look that counts, not how you got that way."

If fear, passivity, masochism, and narcissism are acceptable behavior for women, what is not? The answer is self-evident—anger and aggression. Psychiatrist Alexandra Symonds, among others, believes that certain types of neurosis—phobias, for example—are a way of handling these repressed emotions while at the same time gaining social approval. Phobias, she writes, "immobilize and prevent a woman from any act that might be interpreted as aggressive or self-assertive; in fact a phobia is a statement to the very contrary, since it makes her helpless and harmless." Given no permission to express anger or hostility openly, women "choke off their inner selves" because "healthy growth and self-assertion are seen as masculine." Hence, there is among woman, this time according to Dr. Chesler, "a high rate of depression, anxiety, neurosis, suicide attempts and psychomatic illness in women" as a result of "self-devaluation, inability to express anger, turning in of that anger on self."

The fact that women are most prone to depression (involutional melancholia, the medical term for the condition, strikes one out of ten women seriously enough to require hospitalization) is borne out not only by medical statistics, but in conversations and interviews with women. The depressions they describe are not the "functional" ones that are considered a part of normal adjustment to life's realities—periods of sorrow in mourning, for example—but of feelings of helplessness and the desire to retreat, insomnia, and reliance on alcohol and tranquilizers. Interviewing a group of nine women, for example, I heard most of them describe symptoms and patterns that are clearly recognizable as depression, ranging from such relatively minor evidence as "a feeling of being low, wanting to just stay in and rest," to suicide attempts. Several of the women spoke about long periods of being "sunk in gloom": "I kept going through the motions of taking care of the house and the children, but none of it seemed worthwhile. It was an effort to just get through the day." Withdrawal was a common response: "I sometimes start out to shop or go into town, thinking I just need to get out more, but a couple of times I've simply turned the car around and come home." Anxiety was a common component—not fear of any particular event, but often just a "feeling that something terrible is going to happen" or a free-floating fear of "loss of control."

Many women described particular times in which they felt depressed: "Sunday blues" was common. Most women with whom I spoke recognized a time in the day that was a low point, frequently so difficult that they required pills or a drink. A number of women spoke to me frankly about their increasing reliance on alcohol, verifying through personal testimony what Dr. J. W. Bedell, a California sociologist, had found in a study he made for the National Institutes of Health: Alcohol use by women, particularly those in the middle years, is a hidden but serious medical problem. Several of the women told me that they had observed their drinking patterns changing: "I only used to have a couple of drinks at parties, but now I find that I can't get through the day without liquor." A number of women told me that they preferred to drink alone. Most ominous was the observation "I used to be able to have three or four drinks before I got high; now one drink sets me off," a statement that indicates, according to the physician I consulted about this chapter, that the person has crossed the line that separates the social drinker from the problem drinker and the alcoholic.

A large number of women spoke to me about their dependence on tranquilizers, and many routinely use medication to help control their insomnia. The statistics on the use of mood alteration drugs—tranquilizers, "mood elevators," and barbiturates—consistently show that women in the middle years are heavy users; whether this is because women themselves require the medication or whether it is a part of medical practice simply to mollify us by giving us "happiness pills" is an open question.

The fact is that the hazy demarcation between physical illness, emotional illness, and stress reaction to sociological displacement shows up most clearly in the ailments of women in the middle years, where empirical medical knowledge is obscured by a complex of societal prejudices and myths. Here, for example, is Dr. Jules Henry's interpretation of involutional melancholia, from his essay "Forty-Year-Old Jitters in Married Urban Women."

> Involutional melancholia . . . I learned, was a function of organic decay, somehow related to the female reproductive system; nothing could be done about the onset, though there might be some hope of recovery, just as there was for cancer. . . . The deep depression . . . can no longer be viewed as a simple consequence of physiological aging . . . it must be seen as a disease in which the environment is important, and which is an extreme expression of

a widespread disturbance present in most women as a consequence of aging in our culture.

The consequences of aging in our culture to which Dr. Henry refers are, of course, our feeling of loss of worth as we enter menopause. Throughout our lives our physical well-being has been linked to our biological function—sexual and reproductive—and in a society that so far has not had the imagination to visualize the utilization of women beyond these capacities, women face a serious trauma on many levels when the "change of life" brings us to the certain knowledge that our anatomy is no longer our destiny.

The trauma involved with the change of life goes far beyond the loss of fertility, for in losing our ability to bear children, we somehow call upon ourselves the fear and furies of men—perhaps because society inculcates in men the feeling that only through a woman's ability to conceive their children is *their* sexual potency proved. Here is male rage at its peak, an excerpt from Dr. David Reuben's *Everything You Always Wanted to Know About Sex but Were Afraid to Ask* that author Barbara Seaman calls "so insulting— and so inaccurate—that it's a wonder all the women past forty who bought his book did not tar and feather it, their booksellers and him":

> Without estrogen, the quality of being female gradually disappears. The vagina begins to shrivel, the uterus gets smaller, the breasts atrophy, sexual desire often disappears and the woman becomes completely desexualized. As the estrogen is shut off, a woman comes as close as she can to being a man.

Increased facial hair, deepened voice, obesity, and the decline of breasts and female genitalia all contribute to a masculine appearance. Coarsened features, enlargement [sic] of the clitoris, and gradual baldness complete the tragic picture. Not really a man but no longer a functional woman, these individuals live in the world of intersex.

The change of life in women evokes so much male bias and, perhaps, fear that it is virtually impossible to separate the "truth" of menopause from the delusions and phobias that surround it. Even among those specialists who subscribe to the most "objective" theories about women's health, chauvinism intrudes on scientific assessment. *Women's Choice*, written by Dr. Robert H. Glass and Dr. Nathan G. Kase, directors of the Yale Infertility Clinic and the Yale Gynecological Endocrine Clinic respectively—a book widely recommended by the women's movement for its *pro*-woman stance—contains these lines: "Certain physical and sociological factors enable the male to accept the inevitability of aging. . . . He is less dependent on pure physical attributes to earn a living . . . his position has risen in social organizations. . . . Last but not least, *his sexual appetites and his ability to satisfy them have barely lessened* [italics mine]." This, in the face of overwhelming evidence by the Kinsey Institute and Masters and Johnson that it is the *male*, not the female, whose sexual appetites and abilities diminish with middle age!

Entering the climacteric—the change of life—we are confronted with problems that are at once physiological, psychological, and sociological. Conditioned by society to believe that we are facing the abrupt loss of our physical appeal, that we are about to pass into a no-woman's-land of sexual aridity, we anxiously watch for the sign of dwindling femininity. We are made self-conscious by society's popular image of a "typical menopausal woman" as exhausted, haggard, irritable, bitchy, unsexy, impossible to live with, driving her husband to seek other women's company, irrationally depressed—ideas supported by ads like the one in a current medical magazine picturing a harassed middle-aged man standing next to a dreary woman, with the drug it is selling advertised this way: "For the menopausal symptoms that bother *him* most." The final coup de grace is that if we seek medical care and advice—and most of us do—we will be faced with a baffling confusion of medical and psychiatric opinion about what menopause actually *is* and how it is to be treated. The myths and phobias that society treasures in regard to the climacteric has resulted in a real dearth of information; as *Our Bodies, Our Selves*, a study compiled by the Boston Women's Collective from medical research and women's own experiences, explains, "pitifully little research has been done into symptoms and cures for symptoms of a physical experience more universally shared by women even than childbirth."

What is known about menopause—in brief, the interrelationship between the ovaries' diminishing response to ovary-stimulating hormones from the pituitary, setting off an interrupted cyclic production of progesterone, which in turn causes estrogen levels to fall below the amount necessary to produce endometrial bleeding, or menstruation, eventually bringing about a decrease in the amount of estrogen to which a woman's system has been accustomed—does

not answer most of the questions, for there is no body
of medical knowledge now that enables us to sort out
the relationship between the hormonal changes and
our physical and mental health. What we encounter is
a raging controversy—with one school of thought
insisting that menopause is an "estrogen-deficiency
disease" which can be "cured," while other experts,
Glass and Kase, for example, insist that "menopause is
a physiological phenomenon and not a disease
process." Masters and Johnson state flatly that
"theoretical knowledge and clinical experience
. . . are totally inadequate to meet the requirements of
men and women who currently are living within the
framework of our newfound longevity" and note that
"Personality studies of menopausal or postmenopausal women are more prevalent in the [scientific]
literature than are endocrine studies," citing as an
example the conclusion of Schorr in *Public Health
Reports,* claiming that the emotional complications of
the menopause "are basically psychoneurotic in
nature and are almost always exacerbations of similar
disorder patterns developed earlier in the patient's
life."

As a result of the mythology, prejudice, lack of
scientific data, and presence of theoretical controversy
about what menopause actually is and how it is to be
treated, most women in our society enter the change of
life with the feeling that they are completely at sea, a
situation clearly illustrated at a recent Older Women's
Liberation conference attended by some 500 women,
where, as the New York *Times* reports, the workshop
on menopause, most of the women present seemed to
agree that they didn't know very much about the
subject—and they said, neither did their doctors."

Interviewing women about their experiences with menopause, I came to the same conclusion. The one overriding emotion that women described was ignorance: "I really didn't know what to expect, and I didn't know what to look for." Although all the women who told me about menopause had seen doctors at some time—most of the women I interviewed were conscientious about having Pap smears taken at least once a year—the majority who had gone through menopause had received no medical treatment for it. There were several exceptions; a few had been on estrogen therapy during the course of natural menopause, and all the women who had had hysterectomies had received hormone replacement treatment. It also struck me that the women whose "changes" had occurred after surgery expressed much more difficulty with menopause than those who had not had hysterectomies, but whether that was due to the body trauma of surgery and an abrupt change in hormonal activity rather than a gradual one or whether a hysterectomy is an emotional trauma, I had, of course, no way of knowing.

Listening to women speak about menopause, I heard assessments that ranged from lengthy compilations of physical and emotional complaints— insomnia, headache, palpitations, dizziness, backache, irritability, depression, and of course, the ubiquitous "hot flush"—to: "I didn't feel a bit different, I just stopped getting my period." With or without hormone therapy, a number of women evidently had experienced no discomfort at all. "Menopause is the most vastly overrated 'ailment' in the world," one woman explained.

It was difficult for me to sort out the physical from

the emotional pathology—or lack of it—in menopause. What was very clear, however, was women's comment on the societal aspect of the change. Women were willing to talk about themselves in regard to being, at last, past the childbearing years, and my conclusion was that the "tragedy" of being no longer able to conceive is a larger bugaboo to the society at large than it is to the women themselves!

The fact that the change of life marks the end of fertility did not sadden even one of the women with whom I spoke. For most women, menopause had two tremendous advantages: "What a relief not to have the bother of periods—and thank God, no more worries about pregnancy." The freedom from birth control and its attendant worries was expressed often, with a sense of not only relief, but reprieve. What I heard women say was that they felt their lives had its natural rhythm and that while they had lost a certain "grandeur" in the role of creation, they had also lost their bondage. Pregnancy and childbearing are "iron taskmasters," one woman told me. "All my life I've had the feeling that my body was for some other use than my own. Now, at last, it belongs to *me*."

The change of life, then, seems to be some point of demarcation, but it is a gate through which we go, rather than an exit. Throughout our lives our physical and emotional health has been viewed in terms of society's belief that "anatomy is destiny." With menopause, we no longer function in this "natural" sense as *females*—bound to reproduction, childrearing, nurturing—but now, free from conventional roles, become individuals. We may accept society's definition of ourselves as worthwhile only in our biological function, which means that with menopause we have outlived our usefulness and can expect decay and atrophy. We can ready ourselves for those diseases of middle age which are exacerbated by our turning the energies for which there is no longer any biological or service outlet inward, against ourselves. Or we can take another view of our destiny; by permitting us nearly a half of our lives *after* we have completed our reproductive roles, nature has not abandoned us, but is, in fact, offering us the possibility of another great adventure which society has not yet had a chance to explore.

Chapter 10

THE LEISURE YEARS

To be able to fill leisure time intelligently is the last product of civilization, and at present very few people have reached this level.
—BERTRAND RUSSELL, *The Conquest of Happiness*

"If I'm ever reincarnated," a male friend told me wistfully a few years ago, "I hope I come back as a Westchester housewife whose children have grown up." Visions of sugarplums danced in his head: shopping sprees on a charge-plate, golf at the country club, theater matinees, Caribbean cruises. "Do you think your customers are happy with their lives?" I asked my hairdresser. He glanced appraisingly at a smartly dressed, sleekly coiffed woman in her fifties who was writing a check at the reception desk. "Why shouldn't they be?" he asked rhetorically. "Plenty of time and plenty of money."

The image evokes envy. Our domestic duties are now at a minimum—even those of us who continue to work are relieved of at least one-half of our jobs—our financial positions are secure; our health is adequate. The time of sacrifice is over. One's children are grown, have lives of their own; one's husband is established; grandchildren are dividends instead of responsibilities. We have reached the stage in life in which we are, at last, free to plan our own days, to work half as hard or twice as hard, intermittently or not at all, to follow our own aptitudes and inclinations. The years ahead are bonus years; they belong not to the *others*, to whose health, happiness, and welfare we have devoted all our lives—but to *ourselves.*

What we have now is a new kind of freedom and the possibility of finding creative, satisfying, self-rewarding ways of using our time. What we also have, however, is a stake in what is at best a modern dilemma. Like Sinclair Lewis' tragicomic hero, Babbitt, who found himself suddenly confronting the reality of his fantasy—a week away from work and family to spend in the north woods—we wonder what it is one can do with "anything so heady as freedom!"

The lack of preparation for the leisure years is a problem of our society in general, except for the lucky few of us who are deeply committed to causes, are involved in creative arts, or perhaps have unlimited time and money to be used for travel. But even at that, as one of the women whom I interviewed explained, "People think you need money . . . but more, you need inner resources and a concept of leisure. You have to know where to go or whom to turn to if you are going to fulfill yourself and release those creative energies you didn't have a chance to express before, while tied down to job or home." As women, our problems with the "concept of leisure" are compounded by attitudes fostered in us that make it difficult for us even to accept the idea that we have a *right* to seek out ways of using leisure time creatively.

To begin with, breaking with the habits of a lifetime, in itself, seems a betrayal. Heiresses and guardians of middle-class values, we are inbued with the work ethic; self-indulgence (unless given the excuse of illness) has always been off limits. In a society with little value given to hedonism, we are, much more than any of its other members, bound to productivity, plain living, and high thinking. There is no female equivalent of "wine, women, and song"; for us even the mildest revels are out of bounds. A "night out with the boys" does not translate into a "hen party"; the bride-to-be spends a quiet night under the watchful eye of her parents while the bridegroom has a last fling at the bachelors' party. Women are allowed self-adornment; we can acquire finery—with the understanding that we want to look pretty for *him*—but it is men who treat themselves to expensive toys: sports cars and boats, hi-fi and photography equipment, hunting and fishing paraphernalia.

Self-direction requires the confidence of self-centeredness: "I feel guilty when I'm doing the things I want to do. I wonder whether I'm entitled to be 'selfish.'" Our role in life is "sharing and caring" for others, and we are conditioned toward it from childhood. As little girls we play with toy brooms and dollhouses, while our brothers are encouraged to self-developing hobbies. My brother had a terrarium, a tankful of tropical fish; a row of balsa and tissue-paper model planes that he had constructed hung on a wire clothesline over his bureau. My sons had chemistry sets and stamp albums; they collected coins and did woodworking. I think of the differences between the recreational permission given to the sexes each time I buy a present for a youngster: Boys get cameras and sports equipment, while I have to resist the temptation simply to buy clothes or costume jewelry for the girls.

Interest in an avocation is in itself considered masculine. A girl who spends hours alone deeply absorbed in a hobby that in later life might serve as a source of pleasure and relaxation is immediately suspect. Why does she spend so much time alone?

Shouldn't she be out with her friends, being sociable, getting to be popular? the unspoken question continues. Girls' interests are supposed to be social, frivolous, centered on people: "What does my wife do with her spare time? She talks to her girlfriends on the telephone" (this with a kindly chuckle). Certain hobbies are permitted to women, of course; it's all right, for example, to raise show dogs (a hobby that is approved on the grounds that it is both chic and maternal), and women can have hobby collections, provided the objects are "feminine," like porcelain or miniatures. Women can dabble in sketching and even oil painting, but the serious art collectors are men. Women are not supposed to be knowledgeable.

The final deterrent to self-directed leisure time is that there is always a first priority—one's interests must not take one away from the family. A husband may retreat to the darkroom, spend Sundays on the golf course, disappear immediately after dinner to a basement workshop where he ties flies, but a wife (unless she is making curtains or a slack suit) is not allowed to seclude herself from the family. It's acceptable to "take courses," go to matinees, provided that the activity doesn't interfere with anybody's dinner or weekend plans. An interest that will take her on field trips or, worse, away for overnight is a real problem. A friend who had a lifelong devotion to gardening finally yielded to the temptation to fly to Charleston for a spring garden tour. Her friends congratulated her husband for "letting her go"!

The "permissions" and taboos that we have absorbed through our lives lead us into certain kinds of socially approved avocations. The most popular (an endeavor that occupies some 38,000,000 to 45,000,000 women in America) is volunteerism. We assist in hospitals as Pink Ladies or Gray Ladies, in schools as unpaid paraprofessionals, in nursery schools that are part of poverty programs. We work in church thrift shops; we assist in the "restoration" of historic houses; we plant geraniums in troughs on shopping thorough-fares; we decorate Christmas trees in veterans' hospitals. Volunteerism is a comfortable accommoda-tion to women's role as mother, nurturer, supporter; it is sanctioned by our religious and moral code, as evidenced by the National Organization of Women's study citing the reasons we give for serving as volunteers. The majority of us—38 percent of the women questioned—explain that we volunteer "to help people," while almost another third of us speak of "a sense of obligation." Fewer than one in three names recreational needs.

Volunteerism is a chance to "serve humanity, rather than oneself," explained a plump motherly woman whose activities covered a wide range of church and community service. As a bride, she explained, "I had spare time; there was no need to go back to work. I could take just so much of 'gardening, golfing, and guzzling,' and when the phone rang and some neighbor offered me something worthwhile to do, I was glad to donate my time and effort." The "time and effort" involved serving on membership, program, and hospitality committees—"That means being back in the kitchen!" Although she had been an active volunteer during the years when she was rearing her family ("I say, if someone is willing to be a Den Mother for your son, you should be willing to help her daughter"), she found her real calling after her children left home. "There's no excuse to say, 'I don't know what I'll do when the children are off to school,'" she explained. "I think in the last few years we have been so busy getting we have not been able to give."

The sense of serving humanity again was reiterated by another woman, a stunning blond Long Island housewife, who looked at least ten years younger than the forty-two years she admitted. She found her work with the North Shore Junior League, aiding visiting homemaker services (the league, she told me, serves as a "catalyst" for community action), satisfying and interesting. "The volunteer has a place in society," she explained, because there is "no ax to grind." But her activities, she admitted, *did* fill some personal void; they offered her "a change of scene" and the "feeling of freedom," advantages she could not have if she were in a paid job, which she thought would "tie me down." Besides, she admitted, one of the advantages of volunteerism as opposed to regular employment is that it didn't raise her husband's income taxes!

It is difficult for us to resist the lifelong habit of giving priority to *others'* interests and needs, rather than to our own. We choose to spend our leisure time—hours that belong to us, that might be used for our own self-development—in ways that contribute toward the well-being of our husbands, children, even at the cost of sacrifice to ourselves. We volunteer to serve on PTA committees, veteran's auxiliaries, political groups. We see ourselves as obliged to assist our husbands through our own social skills. "If your husband has an insurance agency in town," one woman explained, "it's important that you be a good mixer, that you know a lot of people. The Civic League is one way to meet them." Rarely do we volunteer for activities that interest *us*; if we are given a choice, we make it in terms of our families or to be agreeable to our friends. I spoke to few women who were enthusiastic about the cause itself; the answer to why each woman had chosen Girl Scouts or Cancer Care had to do with social acceptance or convenience: "They're a nice bunch of girls," or "My neighbor asked me to collect for Muscular Dystrophy, and so here I am!" Nor is it easy for us to shake the lifelong habit of serving in secondary positions; the role of behind-the-scenes helper is agreeable to us. The women's liberation movement has questioned why so many of us are content to "make coffee, not decisions"—and the answer is obvious. The role is familiar and nonthreatening. Particularly in organizations where we work with men—civic associations, for example—we find ourselves more at home and less open to criticism when we avoid executive positions. One is likely not to be labeled as "aggressive" if she takes on the job of recording secretary; how many of us could handle the chairmanship of an organization that includes men—even if, indeed, we were ever offered such a position?

The continuing habit of serving others moves us toward another form of leisure activity: consumerism. At a time when the nest is emptying, we seem to spend an extraordinary amont of time refeathering it. The main street of my town has blossomed with a row of shops with names like Gems 'N' Junk and Franny's Finds. The stores are permanent garage sales, and they are patronized not by young women equipping first homes on a limited budget, but by smartly dressed women of my own age in search of bargains and whimsy. The job of housekeeping expands, according to the Peter Principle, to fill available hours and to use up "splurge" money. I hear myself reiterating the values of old-time thrifty housewives as I compare prices and "shop around"—"I couldn't resist it, it was such a bargain!"

Shopping has another built-in service aspect for us. Having more or less completed the equipping of our own households, we like to feel needed in lending our expertise to our children's domestic establishments. My mother-in-law delighted in buying me the "right" pots and service pieces; I find myself "picking up" a bedspread and set of stainless flatware for my son's "pad." Shopping for grandchildren is a time-honored profession. I have friends who are persuaded that their grandchildren would never survive a Northern winter if they themselves did not make excursions to the stores for snowsuits.

Completing the tally of the traditionally approved avocations for women are what an earlier generation called "ladies' amusements"—cards, bingo, Mah-Jongg Inevitably, the choice of game follows sex stereotypes: There are literally "male" games and "female" ones. Chess, an entertainment that requires logic and concentration, is a man's diversion, as is poker, a game involving high risk and the ability to outfox one's opponent. "Women," writes poet Louise Bogan, "have no wilderness in them, they are provident instead." The only "intellectual" game that is within women's purlieu is bridge, and at that, the classic cartoons are about men's inability to put up with their female partner's dopiness—"Trumped my ace," he explains, standing over the prostrate body of his wife with a smoking gun in his hand. There is a well-known story in bridge circles: Helen Sobel, one of America's outstanding bridge players, was asked, "How does it feel to be the partner of the best bridge player in the country?" "You must ask Mr. Goren," she replied, naming her partner. The story lacks something if one reverses the sexes.

Of all the areas in which sex stereotyping plays its part in leisure time choices, sports undoubtedly heads the list. Physical activity in general is "masculine," and contact sports particularly are off bounds; even as girls we played games by different rules from boys—softball rather than baseball (either, I presume, because we weren't expected to be quick enough to get out of the way of a hard, fast ball or because our arm and shoulder muscles were considered too weak to pitch a ball overhand). We played a diluted form of basketball—three dribbles, remember? We were subtly discouraged from sports throughout our lives by our preparation in school; the sport activities that we would be likely to enjoy later in life—tennis, for example, swimming, golf—were not generally "given" in school, and even after we finished school, there were restrictions against us. Our local private courts are "reserved" for men during prime hours on the weekends ("Women have all week to use the courts," the attendant told me with an absolutely straight face), while the image of the woman golfer—fat and forty, unable to decide between wood and iron, while behind her an endless line of serious male golfers waits for a turn—is enough to discourage all but the most self-confident of us.

Yet, in spite of the fact that we have been made self-conscious about ourselves as sportswomen, there has been generally an upsurge in athletic participation by women recently, most likely as a by-product of the recent trend in medical theory acknowledging the importance of exercise in cardiovascular disease prevention and therapy. Many of the women with whom I spoke reflected this mood. "I've become aware of physical fitness in the last few years," they told me. A number of them spoke about sports for its own sake—"I love the feeling of freedom that I get when I ski down a fast slope" or "the excitement of a competitive tennis game"—but more commonly what I heard was that women were tuning into their own bodies, enjoying the feeling of well-being and increased vigor that comes with exercise and physical activity. A number of women with whom I spoke belong to health clubs, take calisthenics classes, study yoga, jog, or run. Sometimes the activity was inspired by the traditional female reason for exercise—"Stay lithe and lovely" urges the advertisement for a health club in my local newspaper—but I was struck by how many women genuinely discarded the stereotype that requires women to be fragile and sedentary, opting instead for self-development and self-expression through their bodies.

It is this willingness to transcend the limitations put upon us to play the "femininity game" which requires us to be passive, self-renunciative, fragile, and our courage in rejecting our society's pressure to make us "think old," to surrender our rights to utilize the second half of our lives for our own self-expression, that is the other side of the coin for women in the middle years. For if tradition and the needs of our society have conspired to keep us in our place, to require that we forgo the continued living of our lives once we have completed our roles as wives and mothers, there seems to be something within ourselves that refuses to accede to stereotype and custom. I saw this indomitable quality in women first in the area of physical self-expression, secondly with new kinds of work undertaken not for financial reward necessarily, and thirdly in the area of intellectual fulfillment.

One woman, a friend of a professional associate of mine, had spent most of her working life in an office where her secretarial skills were taken for granted and where her competence had actually worked to keep her in the same dead-end job for many years—she simply couldn't be replaced as office manager.' Early retirement opened the door for her; she left her firm, sailed into the offices of an outfit that supplies temporary workers, and found the excitement and appreciation she had missed all the years that she was in the business world. "Wherever I go," she reported, "they're glad to have me. I'm literate. I can spell, I handle my own correspondence. I turn up on time, where I'm supposed to!"

Interested in the story, I called a temporary agency in my area and asked about mature women. "They're very much in demand," I was told. The drawbacks that interfere with a firm's hiring mature women as steady help—pension plan arrangements, for example—do not apply to temporary help. Pursuing this a bit further, I found a few women who were registered with temporary agencies and asked what kind of work they had been assigned. One told me she had worked for a detective agency. "I always wondered what those places did. I found out. Credit checks and cheating husbands." Another had an assignment with a public relations firm that had as a client a candidate for the office of district attorney. "If I could only write a novel! The characters I met!" The option of being able to choose their own hours—"I can work for a month and take a month off if I like"—was part of the attraction; more than that were the sense of usefulness and the edge into a variety of new worlds.

Increasingly, we are seeking to overcome the obstacles to alienation and uselessness that pollster Louis Harris observed in his observations about women in his study of life in America during the 1970's.

> Women are among the most alienated . . . a majority of women (51%) feel that what they think doesn't count very much . . . . Two in five feel they never really had a chance to do the things in life they would like to and probably never will. One in three admits she would like to be more independent, but knows deep down that she can't . . . . One in four feels she rarely gets a chance to enjoy herself.

A great number of women who are moving toward doing the "things in life they would like to"—using these years to fulfill themselves—are back in school, attending colleges and universities which are responding to the demand for adult programs with new scheduling and program concepts. Most of the mature students are not driven by an absolute need to learn a new job skill; the women whom I interviewed are, by and large, participants in the good life, and their reasons for wanting more education are individual ones, sometimes difficult to express.

One woman seemed fairly typical. She had decided two years ago to complete her bachelor's degree at a nearby college, having last attended college thirty years ago. In the intervening years she had reared her family, keeping her interest in art alive by "doing a little painting and going to the galleries." But "in the back of my mind I always felt I had made a mistake in not finishing college—that I had missed something." At first, she said she had a "practical reason for going back to school. I've always wanted to teach." But as she continued, she found deeper motivation. "My aim was to do . . . something that would give me more satisfaction, something I had always wanted, but with having a family, a lot of things got in the way. Now I feel that if I never got a job teaching, it's been worth it. I'm a much better developed person, and I understand life much better. It's been one of the best experiences of my life."

There were other benefits, too. "My daughters were happy about my decision, but I don't think they really believed I could stick in there. I wanted to prove to them that I could. It worked out very well, though; one of my girls was still in college when I started, and there were overlaps in her courses and mine. It was marvelous to talk to her about our courses; it gave us something in common."

The added impetus of a youngster in college was mentioned frequently: "College has given me insight into my children and the younger generation. They are different from us—they're not as materialistic as we were. I listen to kids in class. They're really saying that they don't want to be intimidated. I certainly was at that age." But more often women spoke directly about their own futures, about wanting an identity separate from their family roles, interests to fill their lives now that the children are grown or nearly on their own, and a sense of keeping pace with the changing world. "School makes me feel young again," one woman told me. "It's taking me six years to finish two years of college, and the pressures have been enormous, but it's given me a lot of inner strength. I look back and think that I couldn't wait to get out of high school, and now I can't think of anything I want more than just to stay cn at college! All those books I never read! The excitement of all those new ideas!"

Several women with whom I spoke were aware of the wish to make up for lost time: "Lots of students are just passing through. But I'm getting what I want from college. Life was dull. I was too deep in my small world. Now I accept the value of other philosophies, am interested in other people's experiences."

Listening to women describe their experiences with college the second time around, I heard a number of themes frequently expressed. First, there was the feeling of needing to gain self-confidence: "I thought I'd never be able to compete with those bright kids. I wasn't sure that I'd have the patience to sit in class, and the discipline—or the time—to do the assignments." Two women told me of having been discouraged by "experts." One, during a session with a marriage counselor she and her husband were seeing in an effort to save a failing marriage, had been told, "the ability to learn diminishes after thirty," while another, mentioning her plans to matriculate shortly was told by her physician to "think it over. It sounds like you want to go back to your childhood!" But more frequently women admitted it was their own self-doubts that had made them hesitate: "I just wasn't sure I could do it."

A second reservation that women seemed to have to overcome was the feeling that they didn't "deserve" either the time or money that would have to be invested. It was hard to get over the idea that they were needed at home, even when they knew their domestic duties had diminished. "I'm a wife and mother first," one woman explained, "and if there is any conflict, I have to choose my family above myself."

What apparently seemed to help was the fact that colleges are increasingly geared toward the specific needs of mature students—a movement that has come in tandem with women's increased leisure time. Women and part-time students are presently the fastest-growing segment of higher education, and the U.S. Office of Education reports that about 760 American colleges and universities have instituted programs for mature students. More important is the fact that a number of the programs are particularly innovative, designed to encourage us to return by special accommodations to our needs. "Colleges without walls"—programs in which one can matriculate without attending regular classes, concepts such as Adelphi University's ABLE (an acronym for Adult Baccalaureate Life Experience), which awards returning adults up to 30 credits for their life experience and up to 90 credits to be transferred from other institutions or from study in business or industry programs—are cases in point.

Another plus factor has been the fact that colleges recognize the superiority of mature women as students and have shared that information with women returning to school. "The mature women do much better, are much more serious and more committed than other students," explains the director of Special Sessions at Southampton College. "Faculty members are very anxious to have them in their classes." Listening to women who had overcome the initial obstacle—lack of self-confidence—I heard them express their recognition that they had much to offer. "My psychology professor has picked me out," one of my friends told me with obvious pleasure. "He delivers his lectures directly to me, and every once in a while we share some private joke while the kids in the class look bewildered. I guess it's a relief for him to have somebody in the class with life experience in dealing with people's behavior!"

For some women there has been the gratifying knowledge that their participation in continuing education programs is actually shaping institutions themselves—a point made by one of the members of my consciousness-raising group who is a scholarship student in the women's study department at Sarah Lawrence: "In the seminars, *we* actually suggest the course of study. This is all pioneering work, really, and if the direction doesn't come from *us*, where is it going to come from?" The mature woman as a moving force for change in the universities has also been acknowledged by Dr. Anne Fior Scott, of Duke University, an adviser to the task force of the National Coalition for Research on Women's Education and Development, which is conducting the first nation-wide study of the 500 continuing education programs for women. "Universities are run by men who think the world is divided into disciplines like physics and mathematics. Women in continuing education are organizing courses that women need rather than pulling something out of the curriculum. . . . Women have set the pattern for what men will be demanding in the next fifteen years."

Whether this widespread trend toward continuing education is in itself a solution to the problems of leisure time or just a step toward developing a new ethic of leisure in which people will make the best use of their free time—an evolution that is inevitable with our society's turn toward standard three-day weekends, a lower retirement age, and a longer lifespan—is an open question. "Americans have become experts at work but only amateurs at play," Max Kaplan, director of the Leisure Studies Program at the University of South Florida, believes. "We must tear up the college catalogues and draw up new concepts of leisure, drawing on all aspects of life—political, economic, and social."

Until then we, women in the middle years, whose work-ethic roles end at almost the midpoint of our lives, are indeed finding ourselves, as my friend explained, "pioneering and setting the directions." Without guidelines, by our own abilities to be self-educable, self-sufficient, we are changing the definition of leisure from an absolution of responsibility, its use from a haphazard way of "killing time" to an opportunity for an elective life and a genuine chance to explore and develop new dimensions within ourselves.

Chapter 11

THE SELF-CREATED WOMEN

By this time we can all cite the discrimination and the prejudices. . . . But if we are to go beyond this awakening, we must deal with the ways in which this discrimination has damaged us. . . . We must realize that it has left us without any structures, traditions, or guidelines to support us in the search for freedom. Perhaps the bravest, the most determined and the luckiest of us can make it on her own, but most of us, in order even to start on the road to liberation, need some sort of help. We need suggestions of possibilities. We need to know that we are not alone and that we are not peculiar. We need to know that others have tried, are trying, or want to try.

    —SHERRY SONNETT TRUMBO, "A Woman's Place
Is in the Oven"

I conceived this book from my own need—a search for a way to bypass the dead-end, dehumanizing, and even unnatural role into which I felt I was being forced. As a daughter of my time and place I had never been taught to function as a total, independent being, and the prospect of assuming full responsibility for a life in which there weren't even any positive guidelines, structures, or traditions terrified me, left me helpless. In the beginning, searching for answers, I often found myself despairing. It was not until I began to measure the walls of the prison in which I was living—the dimensions of discrimination against me as a woman in the middle years, the ways in which my society was prepared to wipe me out as a sexual being, as a worker, to misinterpret the messages of my mind and body, to deride me in the media and patronize me in public life, the hundred large and small means by which I was being made to feel ready for the scrap heap at forty-one—that I really began to trust my occasional suspicions that my dilemma was not entirely caused by faults and neuroses within myself.

That knowledge, acquired from a hard look at the very worst of it, was a first step for me. The second step was to find relevant models—to look for the "bravest, the most determined, and the luckiest of us" who were making it on their own—and in the beginning, this too seemed an impossible task. But as the book began to evolve, I sensed something in the air that had not been there when I began my quest. There was a mood, a feeling, that in Bob Dylan's words told me, "The times, they are a'changing

What happened, of course, was that the women's liberation movement had come of age. From agitation for day care centers and abortion and the Equal Rights Amendment to the Constitution, the movement had turned toward the hard assessment of what women's estate actually is. Feminism, like its literature, as Simone de Beauvoir explains, is "in our day animated less by a wish to demand our rights than by an effort toward clarity and understanding." This clarity and understanding are the beginnings of a new awareness that is permeating our society and the lives of women specifically. We are dropping our masks; we are coming out —"up from the kitchen floor," as Betty Friedan writes, "out from the back of the bus," as Aretha Franklin sings. We are talking to each other, sharing our emotions, experiences, we are breaking the unconscious conspiracy that has kept us hidden, and we are beginning to know ourselves and each other.

As we come out, we begin to perceive each other, and it becomes possible now to recognize those "bravest, most determined, and luckiest" women who offer us direction for our own lives by their example, hope, encouragement. Living through the writing of the book in these changing times, I saw them among us—at first, tentatively, for surely, I thought, being *women* they must somehow be fraudulent in their strengths, and then with the surprising joy of realizing that what I was witnessing was genuine.

There are a band of valiant women in our midst who have truly created themselves. Women who see the quality of being female as rich and sensual, who are grateful for the sensitivity that the oppressed must develop to survive, and who are unafraid of the passion and drive that they must use to pit themselves successfully against oppression. They are women who see aging not as diminishing, but as enriching, as a source of wisdom and depth, and the years after forty not as forced retirement, but as a time of exciting "refiring."

I found them first among the extraordinary women of our times—saw them on television talk shows, read about them in magazine and newspaper interviews, in autobiographies.

I saw Helen Gahagan Douglas, whom Lee Israel describes as "a handsome, big-boned woman in white slacks and a gay Mexican blouse, bounding out of her Volvo" to show her spacious, book-lined, and uncluttered house, which is part of a compound on which she lives with relatives. The relatives include three grown children—a painter, a psychotherapist, and a teacher—six grandchildren, her younger brother, and her husband of forty-two years, Melvyn Douglas. In her seventy-two years, Helen Douglas has lived a dozen lives; against the wishes of her father she studied drama, became a star on Broadway, went on to a career in opera in Europe. A political encounter in a Salzburg coffeehouse brought her up against the Nazi ideology, led her to question *"why* I didn't know more about what was going on. I wondered if my own involvement in myself . . . and my talent had left me so that I was isolated in a world that was going to collapse around me. . . . That episode was really the foundation of my participation and interest in the community around me. . . ."

The interest and participation brought her into political life—advisory positions in New Deal programs, a seat in Congress, and finally a race for the United States Senate which she lost to Richard Nixon in a memorable contest in which she campaigned on issues such as energy conservation and ecology, while her opponent whistle-stopped through California explaining that "Helen Gahagan Douglas is pink right down to her underwear." The defeat brought her "freedom. . . . When I woke up the next morning, Nixon didn't have control of my mind." It also gave her the freedom to use the next years to lecture extensively—on issues she saw as "imperative to the preservation of human life": arms control, atomic energy, civil rights, ecology. She wrote a book called *The Eleanor Roosevelt We Remember.* She was presiding officer of the Women's League for Peace and Freedom; she went to Moscow as a representative to the Soviet-American Women's Conference, reporting personally to President Johnson. Her "image" remained through the years of maturity what it had been when Congressional correspondents had tried unsuccessfully to portray her as a "glamor girl"—a serious, dedicated participant in her society whose value increased as her youth was replaced with ripened maturity. "The best way today that a man can flatter a woman, even if she is ninety years old, is to call her a girl. These girl grandmothers are destroying themselves in a senseless drive for something they neither want or need—a youthful body," she told an audience at Hunter College.

What does remain eternally young for Helen Douglas is her own vision, her fresh joy in the world she has helped mold: "I think very often of a phrase that Synge wrote in *Deirdre of the Sorrows:* 'It's a heartbreak to the wise that we have the same things for a short space only.' I get great delight from so many things: looking at the sunset or the sunrise, just seeing the color of things, how the light strikes the trees in a certain way. If I sat here all the time, I could never really take in what I see. I could never see it enough." Age has no weapons against such a woman!

I rediscovered Elizabeth Janeway, whose sensitive novel *The Walsh Girls* I first read while I was in college, now at sixty writing:

> I keep waking up in the morning and thinking I'm 31. It makes me feel like the woman in the laxative ads on TV: "You're not as young as you feel!" I do not find her an acceptable role model, but here I am, missing my real age by a generation. It's not that I want to be 31, nor that I think anyone else imagines me to be 31. . . . In fact, for someone who likes to think she's reality-oriented, it's a mighty silly feeling. So why do I have it?

The reason, Mrs. Janeway explains, "might have something to do with the fact that I've worked all my life in the same field . . . writing has given me a continuous identity." She wrote in college, after she married, when she was pregnant, when she was rearing children, and after they grew up and went into their own careers and marriages, and the work has given her "self-confidence and a sense of self, of being a person who has some value." And as she has used her work, she has used herself, too, for the point is that the continuity she writes about is a flowing stream, not a stagnant pool:

> . . . When I wrote *Man's World, Woman's Place* in my fifties, it was like writing a second first book. I had to read enormously, of course, but I also had to learn quite a new way of writing, with no help from the fictional skills I'd developed in the past. In a way, I think that the willingness to do something like this, to go on learning, is why I don't mock myself more for that silly wake-up delusion that I'm 31. I shall certainly be proved wrong one day, but until I am, I shall think of the work I want to do, the work that lies ahead, *as if* I were 31; I shall be as ready to plan vast projects and tangle with new ideas.

I went to see Viveca Lindfors in a review called *I Am a Woman*—a series of vignettes that encompass a woman's life from the recollection of a first kiss and the memory of a first love to the memory of the loss of virginity, the loss of a husband, and the loss of youth. The play, as Ms. Lindfors explains, "is a collage of one woman's life. I would say that almost anything grows out of my life. An artist works on that principle."

The collage of Viveca Lindfors' life consists of stardom in the Swedish film and theater at nineteen, a career in American movies and in the legitimate theater, three marriages, three children, and an autobiography now in the works. What is the total for her now, at fifty-two? First, a philosophy: "I love those who change in order to stay themselves. That's a quote from Berthold Brecht, and I love it." Secondly, a plan of action: "The women's movement simply started to happen at this time in my life. But for me, it all really began 10 or 12 years ago when I became tired of hearing myself and other people complain . . . I said, 'I don't have to be a victim of society. I can do things on my own. . . . I discovered that if you strike out and do something you want to do, people will come your way." The change involved creating her own material rather than waiting to be offered appropriate roles in the theater and learning to rely on herself after her third divorce. "For the first time, I questioned myself. I had to find out: 'Can I live alone?' I had never been truly independent. I think my experience is similar to that of many women. The equality movement went hand-in-hand with my own dramatic growth." And now? "It *is* dramatic, when you find life really beginning after 50."

I thought of sculptor Louise Nevelson—after a lifetime she describes as "Hanging on, crashing through, loving it all," much of it alone and in poverty, all of it spent developing her brilliant and innovative art—now recognized as one of America's most important artists. "I didn't regret the loneliness. . . . You take your wares and pay your price. In retrospect, now, I find the labor pains have been forgotten or at least rescinded, and now I feel my total life belongs to me."

The life is still working and experimenting, and the woman in the five-story Venetian piazza she owns in downtown Manhattan is still glamorous, outrageous, her own woman. A startling beauty at seventy, she admits she wants "to put on a facade of glamor and excitement. I like to get drunk. I certainly am a free-lance where love is concerned." The sable coat is for trips to the butcher, if she wishes, the chinchilla-on-the-inside, remodeled paisley-shawl-on-the-outside, full-length is coat for gallery openings and charity art events, but the three-inch eyelashes she wears everyday are for herself: "They give me personally a feeling of glamor, even when I'm working." The illusion is part of her style, a symbolic gesture that says one may live vividly, individualistically, and creatively, and that there is no age limit. "I'm here, I'm a great-grandmother. I've done a damn good job, and I'm not finished. Life is a whopping experience!"

I read Eda Le Shan's book *The Wonderful Crisis of Middle Age*—identified with some of it, rejected other parts of it, but perceived through all of it an inspiring woman whose own life I thought held a message for others. Reading an interview about her, I found I was right: Mrs. Le Shan, author of eight books about child rearing and moderator of a television series, recognized herself as middle-aged (a period she defines numerically as being between forty-five and sixty-five and philosophically as the "point at which you recognize that there is more behind you than there is ahead") several years ago, when at age forty-eight she began writing the book from her "own personal life experience." That includes writing her first book at forty-three, beginning to appear regularly on a television show at forty-six, and getting her own program on educational television when she was forty-eight. The "wonderful" part of middle age came, she explains, "when I sensed that being middle-aged and aware of the limits of time, I had to go on growing. . . . When the children are home, a lot of things just get tabled for later. And when they leave, you have the tremendous adjustment of a lot of unfinished business." Part of that "business" was straightening out a marriage of twenty-eight years that had plunged into temporarily troubled waters; part of it was expansion in work; some of it was a letting go, taking the right to become "more eccentric—by that I mean I am living my life and being myself." Her dress, decorum, homemaking standards changed, loosened— but more important than image or even life-style, Mrs. LeShan learned that the middle years make it possible to have "the courage and vulnerability to look inside yourself, find out who you are and give authenticity to what you are."

Well enough for role models, these women who have talent, even genius, whose gifts and accomplishments are beyond the scope of most of us. What about the rest of us? I wondered, and I looked around me at women I knew or knew about, women whose lives had not been a steady ascension into fame, but whose lives were testament to courage, growth, self-development.

Consider Mrs. Persis S. Wilderman, a grandmother who has no legal training, pitted against the former Secretary of Health, Education, and Welfare, Elliot L. Richardson, in a complicated Social Security case brought to a federal court, winning not only the verdict but the lavish praise of the three judges who voted in her favor!

The case—an important precedent for other women in the middle years who may find themselves trying to cut through Social Security's bureaucracy—had to do with Mrs. Wilderman's claim for $900 in Social Security death benefits. The government's argument (which it was willing to pursue through eighteen months of litigation argued in two federal courts and requiring scores of pages of complex legal briefs) was that Mrs. Wilderman had been denied retroactive death benefits because she waited more than one year to submit her claim. Mrs. Wilderman's counterargument was that she had met the requirements—in substance, if not in procedure—by submitting numerous letters and statements during that year. To win, Mrs. Wilderman, a former teacher of the visually handicapped who is now a teaching supervisor in New York City's school system, searched through legal tomes in the New York and Brooklyn Public Libraries and the law library of New York University. Her research produced a twenty-seven-page brief, a thirty-six-page appendix of notes and legal citations, and after the government lawyers had submitted their arguments, a thirteen-page memorandum of reply. It also produced a chorus of complimentary opinions from the judges that included this from Judge Harold R. Medina: "intelligent, right on the ball, extraordinary"; from Judge William H. Mulligan: "She was determined . . . meticulous. I think it's a great thing that somebody can persist and . . . end up in the . . . Courts of Appeals on her own"; and from Judge Walter R. Mansfield: "This lady has the ability to limit herself to essentials and be very calm about it. I've seldom seen anyone before who had the qualities to present an application so that we gained something from it."

I saw heroines who did not make legal history, but

who displayed the same kind of quiet determination and courage, who refused the option of helplessness in the face of insurmountable odds, who determined that whatever life was, it was to be lived on one's own terms.

I think of the North Shore Long Island widow who lost her husband suddenly when he was fifty-two, leaving her with a twelve-year-old boy, an eighteen-year-old girl just finishing high school, and an older boy in medical school. "At first I just wanted to escape," she said. "I didn't want to be in this house anymore. . . . The only escape was work." The work she had done—millinery—was no longer available to her. When her daughter couldn't fill a baby-sitting appointment, she took over, and after that people began calling her when they were going away for a long weekend or a week. "I thought, 'This is my cup of tea.' After all, that is what I've always done, take care of children." Now, with her part-time job as a teacher's aide at the Montessori School, her weekends away— "Most of the families have live-in help, so I'm only there to be with the children"—her immaculate and comfortable house which she shares with a nurse who is also a widow and a long-time friend, her married children's visits, her pleasant and satisfying social life, she considers herself "alone, but not lonely." Her life, as she describes it, is productive; when she looks back, it is with a sense of completion, not yearning for what is lost. Her vitality leaves little time for self-pity. She had seen a Marlene Dietrich special on TV the night before, she explained. Very disappointing. "To me it seemed like she was bellyaching about her age. I felt like saying, 'Marlene, you've had your day. Accept it gracefully.' Now, where did I leave my coffeepot?"

Some of the women I admire have found answers for
themselves in the middle years through trial by fire. I
think of a woman who is very dear to me—my
brother's wife—as she recovered from a painful
breakdown. Through psychoanalysis she was helped
to see that the relinquishing of her own needs for
achievement in order to fulfill an idealized image of
"perfect wife and mother" had taken its toll in a steep
depression; with her therapist's encouragement, she
began the long ascent into self-management: "I
decided my next project was going to be me; if I wasn't
happier about myself, I couldn't be good for anyone
else either."

The first step was a diet workshop, to lose the twenty
pounds she had put on during the depression, and a
course at an exercise salon to get back in shape. Her
progress was so rapid that she was offered jobs in both
places, and for a time she lectured on diet in the
evening and taught an exercise class during the
afternoon. Gradually she worked up to a full-time job
in the gym, became manager. "I realized that what I
loved about the work was the knowledge that I was
helping women to help *themselves.* While I was
working with them, they would talk about their lives,
and I realized that I had a lot of insight into their
problems—I suppose because I had to do so much
probing into myself in therapy. I began to think that if
I had not always had such a poor self-image, I would
have gone into the helping professions years ago."

It took her about a year to decide that it wasn't too
late; in her forties she went back to college for a
graduate degree in psychology, and now, with her
oldest daughter off on her own, her two younger girls
in high school, she has a life plan for herself centered

on an engrossing and exciting profession in which maturity is an asset rather than a handicap. But the benefits go much farther; her growth was matched by changes in her family. As she began to find herself through psychoanalysis, her husband, too, began the journey to self-awareness. Together they went into a marriage encounter group; they "opened" their marriage, allowing each other a kind of independence and self-expression that would have been too threatening in the earlier years of their marriage.

With the raising of my own consciousness, the acquisition of a new knowledge about myself and other women, I tuned into recognizing the signs of self-fulfillment in other women in ways and places I never thought of looking before. A vignette comes to mind: I am in a coffee shop in an eastern Long Island resort early one autumn morning. The restaurant is filled with fishermen who have spent the cold dawn hours hip-deep in the icy surf, pursuing the wily and scarce striped bass. Two women walk in. They are in their middle years or perhaps even past them, their waders and nylon jackets are still wet from salt spray, and their faces are lined and free of makeup, but they are excited, alive. One of them has caught a forty-pounder, and they are sharing the pleasure of a real accomplishment, they are unselfconscious and natural, at ease in the joy of self-expression. A cork-handled knife tied with a bright red bandanna protrudes from one of the women's hip pocket; it is a symbol of the gaiety and sense of adventure that they are radiating—a bright little banner that somehow conveys the whole contagious spirit of their unquenchable zest for life.

Another scene comes to mind—this one more

recently. It is a Monday evening in February, 1974, in my own living room. There are nine of us, ranging in age from forty-three to sixty. We are each having a small glass of champagne to toast the evening, for we are celebrating an anniversary. Our consciousness-raising group has been together for one year.

The group is a significant part of the lives of each of us. In the year we have been together, meeting once a week (except for an occasional lapse caused by ice storms or gasoline shortages), we have truly become a Council of Sisters. We have comforted one member through a divorce and cheered when another began to build a life shattered after a separation. We worried with a sister when her daughter developed a seemingly undiagnosable illness and rejoiced when, just as mysteriously, the girl recovered. We encouraged one of the group to go into her own business—an antiques shop—and congratulated another when she was graduated, with top honors, from college. In the year we supported and empathized with each other as each of us spoke of her feelings and her experiences—dealt with the problems of being women in a man's world and aging in a society that worships youth. We have shared fears about death and loneliness and pleasure in our own and each other's achievements and pleasures. And now, on this February evening, in honor of the occasion, we have chosen for the night's topic what one of us describes as "an uppie"—after all the "problem nights." We are going to tell what we see as the most positive aspects of our lives in the middle years and what we see as the sources of our greatest happiness.

The evening is a *mindblower*. Not a single one of us has said that she has felt *diminished* during the previous year; like the corny commercial, we have all become "Not *older,* but *better.*" Through the year with all its personal trials and all its tragedies, each of us thinks she has found some ways to build a future different from the traditional path laid out by mothers and grandmothers, and each sees herself as having more equipment to "make it" than she had ever believed. From our starting positions—our concern that society had "washed us out" as sexual women and that we were "technologically unemployed" as our children had grown up—each of us feels she has come a long way on the journey toward self-actualization, self-development, and even self-creation.

Some of us have finally severed the silver cords that have bound us to a role that no longer can be the focus of our lives—motherhood:. "I suppose the most positive thing for me this year was the fact that for the first time I was really able to admit to myself that I'm glad the children *don't* need me anymore. My son called last week to tell me that my daughter-in-law had a miscarriage, and I was all ready to go out there and help them. Then he said that he thought they could manage without me, and after I hung up, I realized that until this year I would have felt *rejected.* Now I felt *reprieved.* They know they can count on me when they need to, but I can admit to myself that my job with them is done and my job with *myself* is my biggest interest."

Another has at last given herself permission to accept her own sexuality and is even thinking about turning her new self-knowledge into a career: "It took me fifty years to shake my Victorian upbringing, to stop thinking I had to be a repressed, retiring 'good little girl.' In the last year I've taken courses in psychology, in behavioral science, I've gone to encounters on sexual development. I'm training to become a sex counselor myself. I can see the damage that was done to me with ignorance about my own sexuality; I've become a sexually functioning woman and I see sex as *joyful*, and now I want to help others . . . not seriously disturbed women, but people who need education about their own sexual potential. That's what I think I might have had to give all these years—but it took the women's movement and a break from being 'a mother' all the time for me to find it out."

A third has come to grips with the truth that her work gives her little pleasure and that her relationship with her husband "will never be better than it is now." The positive aspect of her growth during the past year is that she no longer denies herself expression in other ways that give her pleasure: "I've always been happiest when I was outdoors. I love the woods and nature and physical activity, hiking, climbing. It's not an interest that my husband shares, but I've finally decided that I'm entitled to do what I want to with my spare time. I've *earned* it." She had recently joined two organizations, the Sierra Club and a local nature society; her sighting of a snowy owl at Jones Beach was the high point of the previous week. "It seems silly to think that the biggest thing I've learned is that Sundays belong to me—but I guess what it really means is that I don't intend to go through life thinking about all the things I would like to have done but never have."

It is on this note that the evening ends. It has been an emotional experience—and being *women*, we have given free rein to our emotions, expressing openly our affection for each and the gratitude each of us feels for having been supported, understood, and loved in the group. We are proud of ourselves and each other, for without assistance from our society, on our own, delving into our own resources, calling into use the wisdom, skills, knowledge, experience of our lifetimes, we have come to an honest appraisal of our own lives and an acceptance of our own strengths. We have decided to take kindly the counsel of the years, to surrender the things of youth, and to move ahead, fortified, each in her own way, into breaking through the age barrier.

Chapter 12

BREAKING THE AGE BARRIER

If I am not for myself, who is for me?
If I am only for myself, what am I?
And if not now, when?

—HILLEL

It's a curious thing about us—we women in our middle years. We are unique in the most profound sense: *We are the sole members of either sex or any species on earth who have been granted the precious gift of almost half a lifetime beyond the end of our reproductive cycle!* And yet, because our society has not yet come to terms with our uniqueness, recognized our singular destiny, we are tentative, apologetic about our existence. We are, as Elizabeth Janeway writes, "in a double bind. We are expected to feel inferior not only as women, but because we are old."

The key word is "expected." We are not inferior because we are women; our mortality figures alone prove the contrary point. Nor are we inferior because we are no longer young. "How does it feel to be seventy?" Maurice Chevalier was asked. "Wonderful," he answered, "when one considers the alternative." Our problem is that we ourselves have accepted the definitions that society has placed upon us. We have not yet learned how to use our wit, grace, wisdom, imagination, and stamina—the qualities we have developed through all the years in which we have been at the service of *others* for the job at hand, that of creating *ourselves.*

How, then, do we start? On the most basic level, by accepting the truth that *no one can be victimized without her own cooperation.* The deadliest enemy is the one within, who must be taught noncompliance with the enemy outside. We are going to have to change our own images of ourselves and of our sisters, so that together we can develop the measure of self-esteem and self-confidence that will make it impossible for our society to continue to disregard us, to relegate us to the dustbin. Beyond that, we are going to have to work constructively in our own lives to find options for fulfillment in our daily lives—in our work, in education, in our homes and through recreation, friendships, family relationships.

First problems first. We live in a society in which both our public image and private view of ourselves are established by neither tradition nor authority, but rather by the all-pervasive media. We see ourselves and others see us as we are portrayed on television, in advertising, in the movies, in periodicals, and in pop culture. The women's movement has been vocal about the young woman as sex object or domestic dummy ("Rinso White, my ass!" says Sandra Hochman in the grand finale of her movie about the women's movement), but mature women have not yet taken up arms against the "ageism" that accompanies sexism in the media. We are still barraged by the "momism" sterotype—"Please mother, I'd rather do it myself!"—the mother-in-law stereotype, the cranky buttinsky who manages to throw a damper into everyone's happiness in all those dreary situation comedies; the thin-lipped, uptight old maid who is the last bastion of puritan repression, casting a pall of withered old age about her like the spores of chestnut blight. Older women must be presented as positive role models—in the movies, on television, and particularly in advertising. There is no reason why a mature face that reflects warmth, wit, and character cannot sell perfume. Sophisticated Europeans accept the idea of mature beauty; why is the notion so ludicrous in America? For that matter, why does every television advertising "heavy" have to be a middle-aged female moron or nag? Mature women need to organize an Older Women's Media Committee—we have enough buying power to put teeth into it—to make inroads into the youth-oriented media.

We deserve a magazine planned for us. The "shelter" and "slick" magazines—*Ladies' Home Journal, Redbook,* and others—feature articles and fiction geared toward the interests of women between the ages of eighteen and thirty-six; in addition, there are magazines aimed specifically for even younger women: *Mademoiselle, Glamour, Seventeen.* "That Cosmopolitan Girl" is about twenty, even though the vast majority of single women (the marital category that the magazine ostensibly services) are over forty. Granted, starting a new periodical is a chancy venture, but in view of the fact that there are 21,000,000 of us in the middle years, it certainly seems as though there is room for one. At any rate, even if it is not feasible to formulate a commercial periodical of this type, something really professional could be done by volunteer groups. There is a wealth of talent available.

Mature women might exert pressure on the existing periodicals to serve our age group, not by throwing us an occasional bone in the way of an article on hot flashes, but by presenting articles and stories that show a positive image and viable alternatives to the present life-style. Even fashions are a case in point. *Vogue* used to have one downbeat page each month devoted to "Mrs. Exeter" (in her navy blue sheer with plastic cherries at the bosom and a dowager queen hat on her blue hair), but, fortunately, they dropped it some years ago. Since then both *Vogue* and *Harper's Bazaar* have been entirely devoted to sultry Indonesian teen-agers with gold chains across their bare mini-bosoms and accessory ideas to solve the problem of what to do with one's keys and lip gloss as one hops on a Honda. How about a section on dressing *grown-up* women with style and dash ?

Now, on to the present realities of our own lives, our money, work, home lives, family relationships. As a segment of the population which has not yet been officially recognized—in contrast with such subdivisions of our population as "youth," "minority groups," and "senior citizens"—we are going to have to mobilize the institutions of society first to notice us and second to accommodate us. Our first avenue of operation is through the academic establishment. The women's movement has turned a searchlight on the concepts of traditional psychiatry, raising the objection that its concepts are counterproductive to women, for they reinstill the very patterns of self-denial that have handicapped us, rather than aided us in self-development and self-actualization. In recent years behavioral scientists such as A. H. Maslow, psychiatrists including Karen Horney and Alfred Adler, and the sex researchers, particularly Masters and Johnson, have reversed some of the assumptions about women that have been so crippling to us, but we are only at the beginning of this revolution. There has been insufficient research in behavioral science in the area of studying mature women; it remains a virgin field. Even such basic questions as what "the change of life" actually is, remain unanswered. Many universities have initiated programs in women's studies; grants are available for further research. It is up to us, possibly through such organizations as the American Association of University women and our own alumni organizations, to press for special attention to the problems of women in the middle years.

And finally, wrapping up the question of self-image, we have one more untapped area. Such powerful organizations as the Federation of Women's Clubs have largely failed to identify with the feminist movement, mainly because of the age factor. The average clubwoman is past forty, and the issues of the women's liberation movement—day care centers, abortion, and so on—are not relevant to her life. Those of us who are active in women's volunteer organizations need to bring the realities of the situation of our *own* lives to the attention of the groups with which we work and to utilize the public relations aspect of their organizational work into positive self-image. We can take a line from the civil rights movement—Black is Beautiful and so is Middle Age.

The realities of our financial status are consistently glossed over. The myth says older women in America own the major share of real property and other assets; actually, older single and widowed women are the nation's most impoverished group. While the years between forty and sixty are considered "affluent," as workers we are at the bottom of the salary heap; we are dependent on our husbands for support and sustenance in the future. Most of us are woefully ignorant about our own financial situations; we know little, if anything, about insurance, banking, mortgages, investments. Moreover, neither Social Security at the present time nor industry's pension planning is now intended to provide enough money for us to live on when we will need it; the average Social Security check for older women is now $140 a month. In the private sector, only some 5,000,000 retired people are now collecting benefits, a fraction of the employees retired from jobs in private industry. Half the private labor force is not covered at all, and about half of the 30,000,000 employees now covered may never receive the benefits they thought they were entitled to. Because of women's own work patterns of interrupted service and low wages, and because most pension plans do not provide survivors' benefits—only 2 percent of widows receive pension payments—it is women who are likely to be the losers.

Upgrading our financial prospects requires first an awareness of our personal assets and liabilities. If we have left financial arrangements to our husbands in the past—"I don't like to ask him about the insurance," women told me—we must immediately begin to share control. We need to find out what provisions have been made for us, how we can cope with the possibility that we will, at some later time, have to take on complete responsibility for our economic survival. High schools and colleges offer courses in money management; insurance agents are aware of the needs of women and can offer us intelligent advice; our local libraries are a source of information. On the most fundamental level, we need to inquire about wills, safe-deposit vaults, bank accounts. Such action is not morbid; it's simply realistic.

We need to go much farther than that, however,

because however realistically we use our own assets, legislation is required, and it is up to us to make our needs known. We have been accustomed to thinking of ourselves outside the political sphere—women's role in political life in America consists largely of making coffee at precinct meetings and addressing envelopes for campaign mailings. We need now to move into political action; through such organizations as the League of Women Voters, feminist groups such as National Organization for Women, senior citizens, and civic and church organizations, we can press for reform in Social Security laws, tax regulations, and pension plans.

Our employment problems must be met head on. There are "executive placement" agencies for mature men, but so far no one has paid much attention to the mature women seeking employment. How about special placement agencies for us, so that a fifty-five-year-old secretary with everything to offer an employer does not have to run the gamut of general agencies where the emphasis is on providing pretty young faces to status-seeking employers? As a bonus, such agencies also would have a plus public relations aspect; employers need to become educated to the value of a mature work force. On this note, women, too, must learn to protest the turndown on the basis of age as well as sex; discrimination on the grounds of age is illegal under Title VII of the 1964 Civil Rights Act; at very least, we can bring discrimination suits. So far we are flunking out; for all the whooping and hollering by the women's liberation movement, has anyone ever seen a fifty-five-year-old airline stewardess?

Another aspect of employment overlaps with education. The colleges and universities are increasingly working on the problem of continuing education. Outstanding among these are of course, Radcliffe College and Sarah Lawrence, where innovative programs designed to help women return to the labor force have been part of the curricula for some years. A number of colleges and universities offer weekend courses, special summer seminars, and night classes. But on the community educational level, there is much room for improvement. The high school in my village gives "refresher courses" in shorthand, typing, bookkeeping, and computer clerical work, but the doctors and lawyers in the county complain that they cannot get trained legal and medical secretaries. More specialized courses can surely be given in high schools, and it would make sense for mature women to survey the job market, determine where there are openings, and see to it that useful vocational courses are made available to them.

So much for bread-and-butter issues. The challenge of self-creation also centers on our ability to find fulfillment, happiness, and contentment in our private lives, and again, the institutions of society are not geared toward our needs. We are locked into traditional living arrangements, predicated on the nuclear family, and yet many of us either do not live with husbands and children or face the prospect of being outside the nuclear unit at some time in the near future. The woman who lives alone may do so by choice, but for many of us there are real problems of loneliness and the difficult financial burden of maintaining our own homes. The counterculture in our society is experimenting with various kinds of communal and cooperative living, but so far it has been only the younger generation that has shown the courage and imagination to rearrange family patterns. There are possibilities for us, too, to create "extended families," to pool our financial and emotional resources, to reach out toward one another. Even small accommodations can work. Betty Friedan has described a weekend living arrangement that serves her well: Taking over a large house in a Long Island resort area, she and a group of friends have a part-time retreat in which they find companionship and closeness when they need it.

Our living arrangements are based on our vision of ourselves. If we accept rigid social definitions of ourselves, we have few options open to us. The Noah's Ark pairing that requires a woman to be one-half of a unit is unrealistic simply because older women in our society outnumber men, and the figures grow more divergent with the years. Among the built-in assumptions in our society is social acceptance for the pairing of older men and young women, but not vice versa—a notion that is patently absurd in light of mortality figures, as well as what we now know about mature sexuality. Women must reconsider this pattern; May-December relationships make a good deal more sense the other way around.

The two-by-two pairing of male and female in our society is a maddening problem even in recreation and travel. Travel agencies, hotels, resorts have a double standard that until now women have not fought; in many places men may have private rooms with first-rate accommodations, while women have to travel in pairs. We need to envision ourselves as capable enough to manage as independent adults, and we need to insist that we have rights when we travel and dine out.

The entire problem of a satisfactory social life in a society that provides rigid guidelines—a dinner party with the host in charge of the bar and the hostess the food, attended by four or six couples all the same age—is one with which we have to cope. The self-realized woman is not bound by convention in any aspect of her social life—least of all in entertaining, where she may be as innovative as she wishes. Breaking down the stultification of role-oriented recreation roles involves a change in self-image, for we seek out others and make ourselves available to them not only on the basis of what they have to offer us, but on what we feel we have to offer them. Throughout our lives we paid our way in two coins: We were decorative, desirable to others because of our beauty and femininity, and we were valuable for the service we rendered to others as hostesses, cooks, nurturers. Freed from the bondage of both roles, we now have *ourselves* to offer, and at forty, fifty, sixty, we are the sum of our total knowledge and our emotions. What we have now to share is the poetry of experience, with which we can enrich our own lives and those of the people we love.

All of which finally leads us to the road toward salvation that is most easily accessible—the one within oneself. We—women in our middle years—have a number of avenues open. We can stand still, passively accepting the end of our function as society has defined it for us, and drift early into old age. We can go backward, furiously clutching at lost youth. We can cop out, numbing ourselves with drugs and alcohol, or retreat into chronic bad health. Or we can choose to move forward—into bonus years of self-exploration, self-development, self-creation. Each of the choices is dictated, in the last analysis, by our own attitudes.

Last summer I attended a National Training Laboratory program in self-management. The journey into ourselves required that we relive a good deal of our own pasts, a painful task, and the trainer, Dr. John Weir, carried out his role as "father of us all" with enormous compassion, wisdom, and understanding. One day one of the participants in a particularly difficult session, a man in his forties, asked John wistfully, "Where were *you* in my formative years?" John's reply was: "What makes you so sure that *these* aren't your formative years?"

References

CHAPTER 1

HOKINSON, HELEN, *The Ladies, God Bless 'Em*. New York, Dutton, 1950.

HUNT, MORTON, *Her Infinite Variety*. New York, Harper & Row, 1962.

CHAPTER 2

ALLEN, FREDERICK LEWIS, *Only Yesterday*. New York, Harper & Row, 1964.

JONES, ERNEST, *The Life and Work of Sigmund Freud*. New York, Basic Books, 1957.

LASH, JOSEPH P., *Eleanor and Franklin*. New York, W.W. Norton & Co., 1971.

STEIN, GERTRUDE, *The Making of Americans*. New York, Harcourt, Brace & World, 1934.

Additionally, the following novels were used as background material for this chapter: William Dean Howells, *The Rise of Silas Lapham*, Sinclair Lewis, *Babbitt* and *Main Street*; O. E. Rolvaag, *Giants in the Earth*.

CHAPTER 3

BERNARD, JESSE, *The Future of Marriage.* New York, World Publishing, 1972.

FARBER, SEYMOUR M., and WILSON, ROGER H. L., eds., *The Challenge to Women.* New York, Basic Books, 1966.

FARNHAM, MARYNIA, and LUNDBERG, FERDINAND, *Modern Woman: The Lost Sex.* New York, Harper & Brothers, 1947.

KERR, CLARK, *The Uses of the University.* Cambridge, Mass., Harvard University Press, 1963.

McCARTHY, MARY, *The Group.* New York, Harcourt, Brace & World, 1963.

ROTH, PHILIP, *Portnoy's Complaint.* New York, Random House, 1969.

Statistics in this chapter were taken from the *United Nations Demographic Yearbook* (1960), as cited by Betty Friedan, *The Feminine Mystique.* New York, W. W. Norton & Co., 1963.

CHAPTER 4

COOK, JOAN, "The Male Menopause," New York *Times*, April 5, 1971.

HENRY, DR. JULES, "Forty-Year Jitters in Married Urban Women," in Farber and Wilson, *op. cit.*

JUNG, CARL, *The Portable Jung.* New York, Viking Press, 1971.

CHAPTER 5

BETTELHEIM, BRUNO, "Growing Up Female," *Harper's Magazine* (October, 1962).

KINSEY, ALFRED C.; POMEROY, W. B.; and MARTIN, C. E., *Sexual Behavior in the Human Male.* Philadelphia, W. B. Saunders Co., 1948.

———; and GEBHARD, P. H., *Sexual Behavior in the Human Female.* Philadelphia, W. B. Saunders Co., 1953.

MASLOW, A. H., "Dominance, Personality and Social Behavior in Women," *Journal of Social Psychology*, Vol. 10 (1939).

MASTERS, WILLIAM H., and JOHNSON, VIRGINIA, *Human Sexual Responses.* Boston, Little, Brown & Co., 1966.

———, *Human Sexual Inadequacy*, Boston, Little, Brown & Co., 1970.

ZILBOORG, DR. GREGORY, "Masculine and Feminine: Some Biological and Cultural Aspects," *Psychiatry* 7 (1944).

CHAPTER 6

FAST, JULIUS, *The Incompatibility of Men and Women.* New York, N. Evans, Inc., 1971.

LEVERTOV, DENISE, "The Ache of Marriage," in *About Women*, S. Berg and S. J. Marks, eds., New York, Fawcett Publications, 1973.

MCCARTHY, MARY, *Memories of a Catholic Girlhood.* New York, Berkley Publishing Corp., 1963.

ROTH, PHILIP, *My Life as a Man*, New York *Times*, October 3, 1973. Excerpt from novel-in-progress.

SEIDENBERG, ROBERT, "Is Anatomy Destiny?" and "For the Future-Equity, *Marriage in Life and Literature.* New York, Philosophical Library, 1970.

THORP, RODERICK, and BLACK, ROBERT, "Husbands," *Ladies' Home Journal* (July, 1973).

CHAPTER 7

GOODE, WILLIAM J., *After Divorce.* Glencoe, Ill., The Free Press, 1956.

O'BRIEN, PATRICIA, *The Woman Alone*. New York, Quadrangle, 1972.

PAGEBREN, LETTY, "The Working Woman," *Ladies' Home Journal* (October, 1972).

SKERLY, NADA, "Troubled Widows: Somewhere to Turn," *Newsday*, August 15, 972.

SONTAG, SUSAN, "The Double Standard of Aging," *Saturday Review* (September 23, 1972).

CHAPTER 8

BIRD, CAROLINE, *Born Female*. New York, David McKay, 1968.

CARSON, SUSAN, "The Women at the Top," *Newsday*, January 26, 1973.

CULSER, MARGARET, *The Woman Executive*. New York, Harcourt, Brace & Co., 1958.

DE MILLE, AGNES, "Women at Work," in *American Women: The Changing Image*, Beverly Benner Cassara, ed. Boston, Beacon Press, 1962.

JANEWAY, ELIZABETH, *Man's World, Woman's Place*. New York, Morrow, 1971.

LESSING, DORIS, *The Summer Before the Dark*. New York, Random House, 1973.

MERRIAM, EVE, "Women's Expectations," in Farber and Wilson, *op. cit.*

TENNOV, DOROTHY, "The Seven Ages of the Professional Woman," *Women Speaking*. 1972.

WINKLER, ILENE, "Women Workers: The Forgotten Third of the Working Class," *Woman Workers Internationalist Socialist Publication*. Boston, New England Free Press, n.d.

CHAPTER 9

BOSTON WOMAN'S COLLECTIVE, IND., *Our Bodies, Our Selves.* New York, Simon & Schuster, 1973.

CHESLER, DR. PHYLLIS, *Women and Madness.* New York, Doubleday & Co., 1972.

GLASS, ROBERT H., and KASE, NATHAN G., *Woman's Choice.* New York, Basic Books, 1970.

PIGNATELLI, LUCIANA, and MOLLI, JEANNE, *The Beautiful People's Beauty Book.* New York, Bantam, 1972.

RAMEY, ESTELLE, "Well, Fellows, What Did Happen at the Bay of Pigs? And Who Was in Control?" *McCall's* (January, 1971).

RICH, ADRIENNE, Book review of *Women and Madness, New York Times Book Review,* December 31, 1972.

SEAMAN, BARBARA, *Free and Female.* New York, Coward, McCann & Geoghegan, 1972.

SYMONDS, DR. ALEXANDRA, "Phobias After Marriage: Women's Declaration of Dependence," *American Journal of Psychoanalysis,* Vol. 31, No. 2 (1971).

CHAPTER 10

TRUMBO, SHERRY SONNETT, "A Woman's Place Is in the Oven," New York *Times,* October 8, 1972.

CHAPTER 11

AMON, RHODA, *"The Real Suburbia,"* Newsday, June 17, 1973.

[250] THE PRIME OF MS. AMERICA

ISRAEL, LEE, "Helen Gahagan Douglas," *Ms.* (October, 1973).
JANEWAY, ELIZABETH, "Breaking the Age Barrier," *Ms.* (April, 1973).
LE SHAN, EDA, Interview, New York *Times*, March 29, 1973.
WALLACH, AMEI, Interview with Louise Nevelson, *Newsday*, July 15, 1973.